**DATE DUE**

| | | | |
|---|---|---|---|
| AP 28 '88 | | | |
| | | | |
| MR 15 '90 | | | |
| ND 18 | | | |
| AG 21 '96 | | | |
| SE 11 '96 | | | |
| | | | |
| | | | |
| | | | |

# A dictionary of
# ARABIC AND ISLAMIC
# PROVERBS

Other books by Justin Wintle

*The Dictionary of Biographical Quotation*
(with Richard Kenin)

*Makers of Modern Culture*

*Makers of Nineteenth Century Culture*

*The Dragon's Almanac: Chinese, Japanese and other Far
Eastern Proverbs*

*Paradise for Hire* (a novel)
(published by Secker and Warburg)

# A dictionary of
# ARABIC AND ISLAMIC
# PROVERBS

## Paul Lunde
and
## Justin Wintle

ROUTLEDGE & KEGAN PAUL
LONDON, BOSTON, MELBOURNE AND HENLEY

*First published in 1984*
*by Routledge & Kegan Paul plc*

*14 Leicester Square, London WC2H 7PH, England*

*9 Park Street, Boston, Mass. 02108, USA*

*464 St Kilda Road, Melbourne,*
*Victoria 3004, Australia and*

*Broadway House, Newtown Road,*
*Henley-on-Thames, Oxon RG9 1EN, England*

*Set in Palatino*
*by Input Typesetting Ltd, London, SW19*
*and printed in Great Britain*
*by Hartnoll Print*
*Bodmin, Cornwall*

*Library of Congress Cataloging in Publication Data*

*Lunde, Paul, 1943–*

*A dictionary of Arabic and Islamic proverbs.*
*Translated from the Arabic.*
*1. Proverbs, Near Eastern. 2. Proverbs, Arabic.*
*3. Proverbs, Turkish. 4. Proverbs, Persian. I. Wintle,*
*Justin. II. Title.*
PN6519.N39L86   1984   398'.9'927      84–8348

*British Library CIP Data also available*

*ISBN 0–7102–0179–6*

# CONTENTS

*To Caroline Stone*

# PREFACE

Perhaps the quickest way to understand a people or a culture is to learn their proverbs; but identifying and classifying any particular body of proverbs is a task fraught with the utmost difficulties.

This dictionary is a compilation of proverbs belonging to the Islamic world. It is intended for the general reader, the traveller, the visiting businessman. Its provenance is the Middle East and North Africa. Its linguistic bases are Arabic, Turkish and Persian. But all these parameters are in a sense artificial, because proverbs do not naturally keep to their place or even language of origin. The Mediterranean, and particularly the Eastern end of the Mediterranean, has been the crossroads of different world trading systems for several thousand years, and during that time frontiers of every description have changed out of all recognition. It is indeed only in modern times, with the spread and consolidation of Islam, that the Middle East has taken on what appears to be a comprehensive identity. But proverbs are notorious for their disregard of frontiers, be they national, linguistic, cultural, racial or religious. To us it came as no surprise therefore that many of the sayings employed by people in, say, Morocco, were almost identical to proverbs recently current in China, let alone western Europe.

Conversely, although Arabic is the foundation language in many of those countries which have come under the sway of Islam, the proverbial stock of any one of those countries may generally be found to contain its own indigenous elements.

These remarks will, we hope, explain our method of ascription. Those proverbs which occur throughout the chosen geographical area (which corresponds roughly with the domain of Islam, but excluding Pakistan and other Moslem communities further East) have been designated as 'Arabic'; but where proverbs seem, according to our researches, to enjoy a more local usage, then they have been labelled 'Saudi Arabian', 'Egyptian', 'Tunisian', 'Maltese' and so forth. We have also employed two other labels, namely 'Moorish' and 'Koranic'. A 'Moorish' proverb indicates that our original source derived from Spain, where of course there was a large Moslem community throughout the Middle Ages and early Renaissance, while 'Koranic' proverbs have been adapted, directly or indirectly, from the Koran. Strictly speaking only 'Turkish' is descriptive both of a tongue and a country, although the same claim might be made for 'Persian', which we have preferred to 'Iranian'.

It needs to be emphasised that this is only a selection of the proverbs available to us in the many contemporary and historical sources consulted, and it is necessary therefore to say something about the grounds on which the selection was made. On the negative side, we have tended to exclude many 'universal' proverbs; proverbs which are merely variations of those we have included; and proverbs that obviously derive from the Bible and other Christian writings (and these are not insignificant in their number). On the positive side, we have deliberately sought to create a balanced book, one that will provide the reader with a fair spread of wit and imagination as well as the more sententious moralisations which inevitably form a large proportion of any proverbial canon. The search for balance is also carried through into the categories by which we have arranged the proverbs. These we have tried to make as broad as possible (the great joy of many proverbs is precisely their breadth of application); but whereas these categories are presented alphabetically, in line with the requirements of a dictionary, within them the proverbs are laid out sequentially, and not according to any fixed batting order of ascription.

Finally a word about the translations, which are all original. Partly because there were two of us, and partly because of the very long historical period involved (many of the proverbs go back to the Middle Ages, and some are pre-Islamic), there is a variation in idiom and style from one proverb to the next. The older proverbs are deliberately biblical in style, the more recent ones deliberately contemporary. But this is perhaps entirely appropriate, for, along with their many other functions, proverbs tend to preserve language at its various stages of development, and if this book, even as translation, reflects that, then we are glad. Proverbs are considered an important literary genre among the Arabs themselves, and since the ninth century AD scholars and members of the nobility have occupied themselves in making their own collections. The survival of many of these has made this book possible, and gives it whatever character it may have. (An indication of our sources will be found immediately below in the Acknowledgments.)

Translation, however, is as much a matter of communication as it is of preservation, and for this reason we have taken some liberties. 'Allah', for instance, has consistently been translated as 'God', and other Arabic words, such as 'qadi' (judge), have been given their European equivalents. And although there are some notes, we have tried wherever possible to incorporate any necessary gloss into the translations themselves, so that the proverbs, wherever possible, can stand on their own.

*Paul Lunde*
*Justin Wintle*

# ACKNOWLEDGMENTS

The authors would like to make a special acknowledgment to Caroline Stone for help with this compilation throughout its many stages. Thanks are also due to Fusun Chinner, and to Carol Gardiner at Routledge & Kegan Paul. With regard to sources, the following is a list of published materials consulted: *Turkish Proverbs*, Venice, 1844 (no author, published by the Armenian Monastery of St Lazarus); J. L. Burckhardt, *Arabic Proverbs* (2nd edition, London, 1875); Carlo Landberg, *Proverbes et dictons de la province de Syrie* (Leiden, 1883); J. R. Jewett, *Arabic Proverbs and Proverbial Phrases* (New Haven, 1891); Atmarain G. G. Jayakar, 'Omanee Proverbs', in *Journal of the Royal Asiatic Society* (Bombay Branch), vol. 21 (1904); Mohammad Ben Chenab, *Proverbes Arabes de l'Algérie et du Maghreb* (Paris, 1905); A. P. Singer, *Arabic Proverbs Collected by Mrs. A. P. Singer* (Cairo, 1913); Louis Brunot, 'Proverbes et dictons arabes de Rabat', in *Hesperis*, vol. VIII (1928); E. A. Westermarck, *Wit and Wisdom in Morocco* (London, 1930); Edward Robertson, 'Rain, Dew, Snow and Cloud in Arab Proverbs', in *Journal of the American Oriental Society*, vol. 52 (1932); Sigmar Hillelson, *Sudan Arabic Texts* (Cambridge, 1935); S. G. Champion, *Racial Proverbs* (1938); Michel T. Feghali, *Proverbes et dictons syro-libanais* (Paris, 1938); Louis Brunot and Élie Málka, *Textes judéo-arabes de Fès* (Rabat, 1939); Ettore Rossi, *L'Arabo parlato in San'ā* (Rome, 1939); Dayton S. Mak, 'Some Syrian Arabic Proverbs', in *Journal of the American Oriental Society*, vol. 69 (1949); Mohammad Ibn Azzuz Haquím, *Refranero Marroqui* (Madrid, 1954); A. Guiga, 'Proverbes et expressions', in *IBLA*, vol. 22 (1955); Anis Freya, *Modern Lebanese Proverbs* (Beirut, 1958); Bou Qandil, 'Sagesse de folklore', in *IBLA*, vol. 24 (1961); Jacques Quéméneur, 'Cinquante proverbes sur la famille', in *IBLA*, vol. 24 (1961); Shaikh Jalal al-Hanafi, *al amthāl al-baghdādīyyah* (Baghdad, 1964); Tāhir Khamīri, *Muntakhabat min al-amthāl al-'āmmiyāt al-tūnisīyyah* (Tunis, 1967); Ahmad Taymur, *al-amthāl al-'ammiyya* (Cairo, 1970); 'Abd al-Rahman al-Tikrīti, *Jamharat al-amthāl al-baghdādīyya* (Baghdad, 1971); Joseph Aquilina, *A Comparative Dictionary of Maltese Proverbs* (Malta, 1972); Ferdinand-Joseph Abela, *Proverbes populaires du Liban sud, Saida et ses environs. Tom I* (Paris, 1981). Undated: Mubin Manyasig, *A Brief Selection of Turkish Proverbs*, published by the Turkish Press, Broadcasting and Tourist Department; al-Tàliqāni, al-Qādī Abī al Hasan, 'Alū-ibn al-Fadl al-Mu'ayyadi, *Risàlatt al-amthāl al-baghdādīyya*, edited Louis Massignon, published in Cairo; and al-Ibshīhī, Bahā al-Dīn Abū al-Fath Muhammad ibn Ahmad ibn Mansur (1388–1446), *Mustatraf fi kull fann mustazraf*, published in Cairo. Dated *Anno Hegirae* (A. H., counted from 580 AD): al-Maydani, *Majma' al-amthāl* (Cairo, 1352–53); Abu Yahya al-Zajjali, *amthāl al-'awwām fī al-andalus* (Fez, 1395); 'Abd al-Karim al-Juhayman, *al-amthāl al-sha'abīyyah fī qalb al-jazirat al-'arabiyyah* (Riyadh, 1399, 2nd edition).

# A SUMMARY OF CLASSIFICATION

Gardening
Generosity
Genius
Ghouls
Gifts and giving
Girls
Gluttony
God
Good and bad
Gossip
Government
Graffiti
Gratitude
Greed
Grief
Guesswork
Guests
Guides
Guilt
Guns

Habits
Happiness
Hardship
Harmony
Haste
Health
Heart, the
Height
Help
Heredity
Hire
History
Home
Homo sapiens
Honesty
Honour
Horses
Hospitality
Houses
Human nature
Humility

Hunger
Hypocrisy

Idleness
Ignorance
Illness
Imagination
Immigrants
Impatience
Impoliteness
Impossibilities
Imprisonment
Impudence
Inactivity
Incompetence
Inconsistence
Increase
Indebtedness
Individuality
Indulgence
Inevitability
Inflation
Inflexibility
Information
Ingratitude
Inhumanity
Injunctions
Insanity
Insignificance
Insincerity
Insolence
Insults
Intelligence
Intentions
Interference
Intrusion
Iraq

Jealousy
Justice

Kindness

Knowledge

Labour
Ladders
Landlords
Languages
Law, the
Laziness
Leadership
Learning
Leisure
Letters
Lies and liars
Life
Lifestyles
Listening
Loneliness
Longevity
Loose living
Love
Loyalty
Luck
Lust

Male and female
Maltese
Manners
Markets
Marriage
Meanness
Means and ends
Medicine
Memory
Men
Miserliness
Misfortune
Misogyny
Mockery
Modern times
Modesty
Money
Mortality

Motherhood
Mountains
Muscat

Nationality
Nature
Need
Neighbours
News
Night
Nobility

Oaths
Obligation
Occupation
Old age
Omens
Opportunism
Orphans

Paradise
Parasites
Parenthood
Patience
Peasants
Perfection
People
Perseverence
Persian
Personal conduct
Personal reform
Piety
Plumpness
Police
Politics
Possessions
Position
Poverty
Power
Prayer
Praise
Preachers

Sorrow
Speech
Spinsters
Spoils
Strangers
Stupidity
Success
Sudan
Suggestibility
Suitability
Summer
Superstition
Survival
Sycophancy

Tact
Taste
Taxation
Tears
Terror
Thieves
Thirst
Thoroughness
Thought
Threats
Thrift
Time
Tomorrow
Trades
Traditions
Transience
Travel
Treachery
Trust
Truth

Turkish
Turks

Uncertainty
Uncountable
Unfair!
Unwillingness
Uselessness

Vagabonds
Values
Vanity
Vice
Visiting
Volubility
Vulnerability

War
Watchmen
Wealth
Weapons
Weather
Wedding expenses
West, the
Winter
Wisdom
Wolves
Women
Work
World, the
Worries

Year, the
Youth

# THE PROVERBS

# A

### Ability

Ability has no school. *Turkish*

### Abstinence

Practice abstinence, for riches will not last. *South Lebanese*

A lean man who is not hungry is harder than brass. *Arabic*

### Acceptance

When everyone tells you you are an ass, thank God and bray. *Moorish*

### Acquaintances

First befriend the dog. *Maltese*

He whom you know is better than he whom you do not know. *Tunisian*

(*Note* A similar Tunisian proverb goes 'The worst of those whom you know is better than the best of those you do not know.')

*See also* Companions, Friends

## Acre

What does Acre care for the swell of the sea? *Lebanese*

## Actions

The planting of one tree is worth the prayers of a whole year. *Turkish*

Good deeds cut off tongues. *Arabic*

In haste is regret, in slowness peace. *Tunisian*

## Adaptability

That which bends does not break. *South Lebanese*

Throw a man into the sea and he will become a fish. *Tunisian*

He who changes his ways loses his happiness. *Syrian*

## Advantage

The foot that is too swift must be cut off. *Judaeo-Arabic*

## Advice

Good advice is worth a camel. *Lebanese*

Seek advice from the old, and then do the opposite. *Tunisian*

Too much advice gives rise to enmity. *Tunisian*

Ask advice from a thousand men; ignore the advice of a thousand more; then go back to your original decision. *Lebanese*

Too much advice and the suspicion arises: what does he want? *Medieval Arabic*

The man who follows his wife's advice will never look on God's face. *Maltese*

## Africa

The man who has drunk once from the springs of Africa will drink from them again. *Arabic*

## Ageing

When you reach forty a new ailment is suffered every year. *Arabic*

## Aggregation

One hair added to another makes a beard. *Lebanese*

## Alcohol

For every bottle there is a cork.   *Maltese*

The man who wants to get drunk does not count the glasses. *Medieval Arabic*

When a drunkard smells a pomegranate he wants it to sin. *Medieval Arabic*

How can the cask be full when the wife is drunk? *Maltese*

## Ambassadors

An ambassador suffers no fall. *Turkish*

## Ambition

To get what you want you must be prepared to kiss a dog on its mouth. *Tunisian*

Wield your sword and become an Emir; feed the poor and become a Shaikh. *Lebanese*

Climb like a cucumber, fall like an aubergine. *Arabic*

He who rides a horse of wind with legs of wax melts in the sun. *Maltese*

If you fall in love, fall in love with a prince; if you steal, steal silk; and if you knock at a door, knock at the door of a great man, so that when they revile you it will be for something big. *Lebanese*

No tree has ever reached the sky. *Syrian*

Every falcon dies with his eye fixed on his prey. *Arabic*

The camel that looks for horns will lose his ears. *Turkish*

Stretch your feet only as your blanket allows. *Turkish*

Every illiterate dreams of being prime minister. *Turkish*

To lick the sky with the tongue. *Arabic*

(*Note*   A common proverbial expression carrying the same meaning as 'reach for the moon'.)

If you can't get what you want, want what you can get! *Lebanese*

## Anger

Sweeter than honey is anger. *Turkish*

A beggar's ire falls on his own head. *Persian*

An angry man is a madman's brother. *Lebanese*

## Anxiety

In this world only three things dispel anxiety: women, horses and books. *Arabic*

A candle does not dispel the gloom of anxiety. *Moorish*

If you have anxieties, go to sleep. *Moorish*

*See also* Worries

## Appeasement

Until you have reached the other side of the bridge go on calling the bear 'uncle'. *Turkish*

## Appearances

Not everything round is a nut, not everything long is a banana. *Lebanese*

The oleander is beautiful, the oleander is bitter. *Moroccan*

The house may be imposing, but God knows what is inside it. *Omani*

An impotent man and a barren woman: where does the child come from? *Moorish*

Not everyone with a black face says 'I am a blacksmith'. *Tunisian*

Eat what you like, but dress like everybody else. *South Lebanese*

## Arabs

An Arab's intelligence is in his eyes. *Arabic*

## Arbitration

He who tries to reconcile two adversaries receives two-thirds of the blows. *Lebanese*

## Armenians

God created serpents, rabbits, and Armenians! *Turkish*

Anyone who can cope with an Armenian can cope with the devil. *Persian*

## Arrogance

The arrogant man has no friends. *Medieval Arabic*

If anyone shits in your hand fling it in his face. *Maltese*

Bulls stumble in the houses of mice. *Saudi Arabian*

Better to be wrong with everyone than right by yourself.
*Moorish*

When a chicken gives the call to prayer, slaughter
it.   *Moorish*

### Artistic temperament

There's no point in asking a singer to sing or a dancer
to dance. *Lebanese*
(*Note*   I.e. because they certainly won't oblige.)

### Astrology

It is a lazy man who becomes an astrologer. *Arabic*

### Authority

One rug can accommodate ten dervishes, but there is no
kingdom that can accommodate two kings. *Persian*

A hundred years of tyranny is preferable to one night of
anarchy. *Arabic*

The Sultan is cursed in his absence. *Egyptian*

Better to rule devils than be ruled by angels. *Maltese*

If you wish to be obeyed don't ask the
impossible. *Medieval Arabic*

The sword does not cut its own sheath. *Turkish*

Two swords cannot fit in one scabbard; two Sultans
cannot rule at the same time. *Omani*

Shit falls downward. *Lebanese*

An ass is an ass, even when it carries the Sultan's treasure. *Lebanese*

The man who is right is Sultan. *Lebanese*

Better the tyranny of the cat than the justice of the mouse. *Lebanese*

When the prince starts singing troubles are beginning. *Moorish*

Amongst the blind, the one-eyed is Pasha. *Moorish*

Better the tyranny of the believer than the justice of the infidel. *Tunisian*

He who eats the Sultan's raisins must give him dates. *Tunisian*

Though he wears a crown, one man's needs are the same as another's. *Arabic*

The eye cannot prevail over the awl. *Lebanese*

*See also* Justice, Law, Power

### Avarice

God despises two things, and the better of the two is avarice. *Arabic*

If the son of Adam had two rivers full of wealth, he would weep for a third. *Arabic*

Today you give me wool, tomorrow you take my sheep. *Egyptian*

*See also* Greed

# B

## Bachelors

Every bachelor is a sovereign. *Turkish*

An unmarried man is Satan's brother. *Tunisian*

## Bad influences

Be guided by the crow and you will come to the body of a dead dog. *Arabic*

## Bad language

Spit cannot return to the mouth. *Moroccan*

## Beards

No beard, no authority. *Turkish*

It is better to meet a Jew early in the morning than a man with no beard. *Lebanese*

## Bears

All the nine songs known to bears are about wild pears. *Turkish*

(*Note*  A variant of this proverb gives honey in place of wild pears.)

## Beauty

Beauty is beauty, drunk or sober. *Moorish*

Everything beautiful has a flaw. *Tunisian*

A thousand dogs do not make a gazelle. *Iraqi*

Better than beauty is a camel. *Medieval Arabic*

## Bedouin

To the Bedouin everything is a piece of soap. *Arabic*

The fortunes of the Arabs who wear sandals have been eaten by the Arabs who wear slippers. *Arabic*

(*Note*  This proverb is a slur on townsfolk, i.e. those who wear slippers.)

Bid good day to a Bedouin and already you have lost a loaf of bread. *Moroccan*

The Bedouin use their beards for soap. *Lebanese*

After forty years the Bedouin took revenge and said: 'I have been quick about it!' *Lebanese*

Do not show a Bedouin or a rat the door of your house.
*Tunisian*

## Beggars

Let one beggar marry another and all you will get is
more beggars. *Lebanese*

## Benevolence

He who does good to me and evil to others is the king
of benefactors. *Lebanese*

*See also* Charity

## Bereavement

It is easier to be a bachelor all your life than a widower
for a month. *Lebanese*

## Birth

Birth is the messenger of death. *Arabic*

Two midwives give the child a crooked head. *Persian*

## Blackamoors

He who would wash a blackamoor soon gets rid of his
soap. *Turkish*

## Blindness

If you meet a blind man, throw him on the ground and steal his lunch, for you are not more merciful than God. *Lebanese*

The blind man shits on the roof of the house and thinks nobody knows. *Lebanese*

The man with one eye is not blind. *Lebanese*

There is no blindness except blindness of heart. *Tunisian*

## Boastfulness

The bald-headed woman boasts of her cousin's hair. *Lebanese*

Boasting of one's merits is better than boasting of one's pedigree. *Arabic*

They said 'Our bread is bigger than your bread', and we said 'Give us some!' *Lebanese*

## Books

A book in the pocket is a garden in the pocket. *Arabic*

It is for its contents that one kisses a book. *Arabic*

## Bravado

He who makes light of other men will be killed by a turnip. *Lebanese*

14

## Bravery

Flight is two-thirds of valour. *South Lebanese*

Ten marks for bravery, nine marks for strategy. *Turkish*

## Buildings

The new building should be rented to your enemy. *Maltese*

(*Note* A longer version of this proverb runs: First rent a new house to your enemy, then to a relative, and only then live in it yourself.)

May God afflict you with the services of a carpenter, a house-painter and a mason. *Lebanese*

Construction is a ghoul. *Lebanese*

## Business

When business is booming slaughter your dog. *Lebanese*

Do not turn a hen into broth if its chicks have golden feathers. *Syrian*

You can't carry two watermelons in one hand. *Arabic*

It is better to have a thousand employees who steal than one partner with whom you have to settle accounts. *Lebanese*

Your partner is your opponent. *Egyptian*

A contract in the field is better than a quarrel on the threshing floor. *Moroccan*

*See also* Commerce

# C

### Camels

No camel knows of God until he dies. *Arabic*

It is better to endure the wind of a camel than the prayers of a fish. *Arabic*

Only the milk thistle can satisfy the camel. *Arabic*

He who becomes a camel driver must raise the door of his house. *Syrian*

### Chance

One tiny insect may be enough to destroy a country. *Medieval Arabic*

*See also* Consequences

### Change

O God, spare us from change. *Tunisian*

### Character types

A face cleaned by the butcher's sponge. *Turkish*

A face that wouldn't smile at warm bread. *South Lebanese*

He'd burn down a city to light a cigarette. *Lebanese*

16

As tall as a bean with the voice of a ghoul. *Tunisian*

A swelling paunch, a treacherous heart. *Medieval Arabic*

Like the cornered snake he bites his own belly. *Arabic*

He wears his secret in a sling. *Arabic*

(*Note*   i.e. for all to see.)


Like a dog in the stable, he won't eat, neither will he let the ass eat. *Arabic*

He pricks himself on the thorns of a cucumber. *Lebanese*

It's the goat that has mange which will only drink from the head of the fountain. *Arabic*

Afraid to shit in case he feels hungry. *South Lebanese*

(*Note*   This is usually said of a miser.)

Smile at him and he brings his donkey in as well.
*Lebanese*

His words are like farting on a stone floor. *Lebanese*

He could find fault with a bird on the wing. *Lebanese*

He can swallow a camel but chokes on a mosquito.
*Lebanese*

(*Note*   A similar Lebanese saying is 'He can swallow the sea but baulks at a rivulet'.)

Hit on the head his brains popped out at his knees.
*Omani*

The beard is full, the brain is lean. *Tunisian*

A man with a big nose is a man of standing. *Lebanese*

Couldn't tell a pistacchio from a hazelnut, or a bath from a hotel. *Tunisian*

Afraid of the shadows of his own ears. *Lebanese*

He trips over cigarette ash. *Lebanese*

Just like a goat, they bleat from afar and butt when they are near. *Tunisian*

## Charity

Do good and throw it in the sea. *Moorish*

The man who weeps for all soon loses his eyes. *Turkish*

Do good and be rewarded with evil. *Lebanese*

## Cheats

The man who cheats you once will cheat you a hundred times. *Arabic*

## Childbirth

Forty midwives cannot prevent a woman's labour. *Turkish*

## Children

There is no light in the house where there are no children. *Syrian*

A child is child, even if he is the son of a prophet.
*Lebanese*

(*Note* Another Lebanese proverb concludes 'even if he is the ruler of a city'.)

He who has children has torments. *Tunisian*

The wish for children is better than the wish for money.
*Tunisian*

It is a great advantage to have many hands at the harvest; it is a great calamity to have many hands at the table.
*Lebanese*

A wise child is better than an old fool. *Lebanese*

To act as judge between children is to hang oneself.
*Lebanese*

No one ever tires of tea and their parents' blessing.
*Moroccan*

Tickle its chin and the child forgets its mother. *Moroccan*

Ticks, bed-bugs and a crying child are insupportable.
*Lebanese*

An annoying child brings curses on his family. *Egyptian*

When the child falls silent mischief follows. *Arabic*

*See also* Parenthood, Relatives (Sons and Daughters)


## Christians

Be nice to Christians when you need them, but otherwise bring a wall down on their heads. *Lebanese*

19

He who has seen the land of the Christians has wasted his days. *Moroccan*

A thing can only be well done if a Christian has had a hand in it. *Moroccan*

Carry Christian dung, but never beg Christian alms. *Moroccan*

Dine with a Jew, but seek shelter from a Christian. *Arabic*

Sleep with a Christian and she'll take everything you've got. *Moroccan*

Red-headed people should not be sought, bought or sold, but driven away. *Turkish*

The head of a Greek Orthodox Christian cannot be smashed even with a sharp axe. *Lebanese*

## Circumstances

A thoroughbred horse is not dishonoured by its saddle. *Syrian*

When you see someone sitting in the street you know it is better than his house. *Moorish*

## Cleanliness

Either it's clean enough to pray upon, or dirty enough to be thrown away. *Omani*

## Coffee

One cup of coffee, forty years' friendship. *Turkish*

Coffee without tobacco is like a Jew without a rabbi.
*Moroccan*

## Cold

Cold as the locust on the dew. *Palestinian*

## Commerce

Commerce doesn't mix with astrology. *South Lebanese*

Gold is polished with bran. *South Lebanese*

(*Note*  I.e. cannot be gained without sweat.)

The man with wheat has no sacks, the man with sacks has no wheat. *Maltese*

When a ewe dies in Makran, the price of butter does not go up in Oman. *Omani*

Vinegar at a good price is sweeter than honey. *Arabic*

It is better to make a profit on dirt than a loss on musk. *Arabic*

When a merchant criticises the merchandise it is because he wants to buy it. *Arabic*

He who pays cash will be treated like a partner. *Persian*

When one buys cloth it is not measured against one's own ell. *Turkish*

An ass's load does not include the saddle. *Turkish*

Big fish eat little fish. *Lebanese*

Buy and sell, and your name will not perish. *Iraqi*

Whether you lend or borrow, you will sink without trace. *South Lebanese*

Send your money to do your bidding, and stay at home. *Tunisian*

The townsman gets the livelihood, the Bedouin gets the profit. *Tunisian*

Give credit, and lose your merchandise; ask for payment and get an enemy. *Syrian*

Start selling shrouds and people will stop dying. *South Lebanese*

Fraternise like brothers, but do business like strangers. *South Lebanese*

The bazaar recognises neither father nor mother. *Turkish*

*See also* Business

## Companions

Falcon with falcon, goose with goose, and bald hen with lame cock. *Turkish*

Gold buttons cannot belong to a torn coat. *Turkish*

## Compassion

Even the hand of compassion is stung when it strokes a scorpion. *Persian*

## Compliance

When the ship is sinking, jump on its rudder. *Moorish*

(*Note* This will make the ship sink faster.)

## Complaint

The loudmouth goes to hell and complains that the wood is green. *South Lebanese*

Complain to the bow and it will send you an arrow. *Arabic*

## Compromise

Too soft, and you will be squeezed; too hard, and you will be broken. *Arabic*

If you are blind and deaf, smell the odour of the paint. *Arabic*

Better peace than having to make peace. *Maltese*

## Concentration

The man who looks up is the man who gets tired. *Lebanese*

## Conditioning

He who keeps company with the unshod forgets his shoes. *Tunisian*

## Conformity

Among the one-eyed close one eye. *Arabic*

(*Note* A Turkish proverb of similar import runs: 'Keep your eyes closed among the blind.')

To avoid being eaten by wolves be a wolf! *Tunisian*

If you go to a country where they worship the calf, pick grass and feed it. *South Lebanese*

Do as your neighbour does or shut the door. *Tunisian*

## Consensus

If two people tell you your head is missing, touch it and see. *Sudanese*

## Consequences

After the fire, ashes; after the rain, roses. *Moroccan*

One rope, one acrobat. *Turkish*

He who plays with cats must bear the scratches. *Algerian*

If you drive an ass you must suffer its wind. *Arabic*

When the snow melts, the shit appears. *Lebanese*

Feed him a pin and he shits a needle. *South Lebanese*

The barking of a dog cannot harm the clouds. *Tunisian*

A nail may save the horseshoe, the horseshoe may save the horse, the horse may save the rider, and the rider may save the kingdom. *Turkish*

## Consolation

When things get rough, visit the graveyard. *Tunisian*

## Constantinople

Constantinople is a place where fire takes your goods, plague takes your life, and women take your wits. *Turkish*

## Contentment

He who has never seen meat is happy with tripe. *Omani*

A hedgehog and peace is better than a gazelle and grief. *Moroccan*

(*Note* Throughout Arabic cultures the gazelle is a symbol for the beautiful woman.)

Measure your guilt, then stretch your legs. *Egyptian*

The sweetness of rest comes from the bitterness of labour. *Algerian*

Everyone is pleased with his brains; no one is pleased with his wealth. *Omani*

The moon is our lantern, onions our apples. *Maltese*

A glass of tea at dawn is better than a hundred camels in the pasture. *Tunisian*

Praise be to Him who made men content with their intelligence! *Lebanese*

An overbundance of good things is no cause to repine. *Tunisian*

He who is not satisfied at his father's table will never be satisfied. *South Lebanese*

If you love the moon, ignore the stars. *Moorish*

Better to ride a dung-beetle than tread on soft carpets. *Arabic*

Now that the pumpkin is large and round it has forgotten its past. *Lebanese*

A bird in the hand is worth ten on the roof. *Tunisian*

My bread is baked, my jar is full. *Arabic*

The dead are content. *Tunisian*

*See also* Discontentment, Happiness


## Conversation

The words of the night are butter which will melt in the morning. *Tunisian*

If speech were silver, silence would be golden. *Tunisian*

When I saw you I knew half of you; when we spoke I knew everything. *Maltese*

*See also* Silence, Speech


## Co-operation

It is by helping one another that the lion is subdued. *Moroccan*

## Co-ownership

A shared pot doesn't boil. *Omani*

## Correction

Are the eyebrows to be corrected by pulling out the eyes? *Turkish*

## Corruption

May God protect the vineyard from its watchman! *Lebanese*

To destroy the cobweb, destroy the spider. *Maltese*

When cat and rat join forces the country is destroyed. *Omani*

A bribe removes the turban from a judge. *South Lebanese*

It is from the head that the fish first stinks. *Turkish*

(*Note* I.e. corruption begins at the top.)

He who does not eat garlic does not smell of it. *Lebanese*

The more devils that disappear, the easier it is for the angels. *Arabic*

## Courtesy

It is from the discourteous that the courteous learn courtesy. *Turkish*

27

## Cowardice

The coward survives to raise his children. *Sudanese*

When the wolf attacks, the dog hides. *Lebanese*

## Craftsmanship

Craftsmanship spouts gold. *Arabic*

## Crime

Nobody steals a minaret unless they know where to hide it. *Arabic*

The man who goes to market with nothing in his pockets is a thief. *Sudanese*

Gaol for men, weeping for women.  *Lebanese*

The thief makes a profit on everything he sells. *Omani*

He who steals an egg will steal a camel. *Arabic*

*See also*   Thieves

## Cunning

What the rat cannot reach with its tongue it takes with its tail. *Maltese*

Cleverness wins over strength. *Omani*

A man without cunning is like an empty matchbox. *Omani*

## Curiosity

An inquisitive dog does not keep good watch. *Tunisian*

## Curses

Even a curse, at the right moment, is like praising God.
*Lebanese*

## Customs

Customs are a fifth element in the world. *Syrian*

(*Note* I.e. along with earth, fire, air and water.)

# D

### Danger

When danger approaches, sing to it. *Arabic*

### Death

Death is a dark camel that kneels at every man's gate. *Arabic*

The sound of footsteps does not disturb the severed head. *Tunisian*

The cemetery never rejects a corpse. *Lebanese*

The corpse-washer cannot guarantee paradise. *Omani*

The cock dies with its eyes fixed on the dung-heap. *Lebanese*

When a blind man dies his eyes become almonds. *Turkish*

Death veils all faults. *Iraqi*

He who sees a dead man is thankful to be alive. *Tunisian*

The wailing is great, but the corpse is a mouse. *Tunisian*

No one laments the death of a suicide. *Sudanese*

When the elephant dies, its bones become souvenirs.
*Iraqi*

When the ant grows wings it is about to die. *Arabic*

Whoever returns with news of the tomb? *Arabic*

Better to be devoured by a lion than eaten by a dog.
*Lebanese*

People who weren't invited to the wedding won't attend
the funeral. *Arabic*

Even the dead goat has a stiff tail. *Turkish*

The death of a djinn is relief to the angels. *Moroccan*

A boat stranded for ten centuries may float again, but
love and death are without recourse. *Arabic*

Bury your dead and return to your Lord. *Tunisian*

The Lord of Death fears death. *Arabic*

The last to die is the King of Death. *Moorish*


**Debts**

Debt is a chain on a man's wrists. *Lebanese*

Owe nothing to the rich man, and be owed nothing by
the poor man. *Turkish*

Your creditor is your Sultan. *Moroccan*

A debt of just two piastres is enough to blacken your
face. *Moroccan*

## December

December and January are the stallions of winter. *Arabic*

## Deception

The biggest nuts are the empty ones. *Moroccan*

A fig tree with figs turned out to be a ruin with mosquitoes. *Moroccan*

Do not suppose a man can cook just because you see him blowing on the fire. *Lebanese*

You put a burning coal in my ear and say 'Smell the roasting meat!' *Lebanese*

## Delusions

Who does not think that his fleas are gazelles? *Arabic*

## Dependence

The greatest curse is to need help from others. *Maltese*

He who is used to eating your bread cannot look at your dough without feeling hungry. *Arabic*

## Desires

The well is deep, the rope is short. *Arabic*

He who loves prickly pears must not fear thorns, and he who loves a married woman must not fear death. *Maltese*

The thing dearest to the heart of man is that which is forbidden him. *Arabic*

Of all things you covet, money is the best. *South Lebanese*

When you have something in your hand, its charm flees. *Iraqi*

## Desperation

As a last resort the octopus will eat its fingers. *Maltese*

What drowning man would not cling to the tail of a serpent? *Turkish*

The drowning man clutches the ropes of the wind. *Lebanese*

The man who needs fire will hold it in his hands. *Arabic*

## Destiny

No water can wash away the destiny written on a man's forehead. *Moroccan*

Destiny caresses the few and molests the many. *Turkish*

Every sheep will hang by its own foot. *Turkish*

Wherever it grows, wheat always arrives at the millstone. *Arabic*

Circling about to reach Paradise is better than going straight to Hell. *Moorish*

When the rings are gone, the fingers remain. *Moorish*

## Discipline

Where the teacher strikes roses will grow. *Turkish*

You can train anything, except a wolf and a child. *Tunisian*

The cudgel comes from Paradise. *Tunisian*

## Discontent

The camel carries the load, but it is the tick that complains. *Moroccan*

The neighbour's cooking always smells better. *Maltese*

## Discretion

The eye has a veil. *Arabic*

## Discrimination

If a man gives one child an extra date, God shall give him a burning coal. *Lebanese*

## Dishonour

Fight for honour, for dishonour is easily won. *Arabic*

## Distress

Distress turns the lion into a fox. *Persian*

## Division

Divide the sea and you'll wind up with ditches. *Moroccan*

## Dogs

The campsite without dogs is an empty place. *Tunisian*

One dog faced with two dogs is a coward; one dog faced with three dogs is dead. *Arabic*

There's no fat on a dog's tail. *Kurdish*

## Dreams

Day denies the promises of night. *Lebanese*

## Dress

Clothes that protect you from the cold will protect you from the heat. *Arabic*

A gazelle needs no ornaments to be beautiful. *Yemeni*

Silk goes with everything. *Iraqi*

(*Note* From Baghdad.)

## Dwarfs

Steer clear of dwarfs, for God has seen fit to strike them on the head. *Turkish*

# E

## Ease

Until you have walked across the sands, do not sleep in sheets of silk. *Arabic*

## Eavesdropping

Walls have mice, and mice have ears. *Persian*

(*Note* The proverb 'Walls have ears' has been universal since the Middle Ages, but this ancient Persian version perhaps explains its origin.)

## Education

It is with blows that the bear learns to dance. *Syrian*

Repetition teaches the donkey. *Saudi Arabian*

Don't bother about educating your son: life will teach him. *Lebanese*

*See also* Learning

## Egotism

His mother was an onion, his father garlic, and yet he is a rose! *Turkish*

Big head, big headache. *Turkish*

## Embarrassment

As embarrassed as a Jew in a mosque. *Omani*

## Enemies

Better a thousand dogs barking for you than one barking at you. *Arabic*

In every enemy that is an ant, behold an elephant. *Turkish*

Love in secret, but flatter him you hate. *Egyptian*

A thousand friends are few, one enemy is many. *Algerian*

The man who accepts the word of his enemy is doomed. *Arabic*

Friends inspect the head, enemies the feet. *Turkish*

If you really want to annoy your enemy, keep silent and leave him alone. *Arabic*

An intelligent enemy is better than an ignorant friend. *Arabic*

I am sick because of you, and you visit me in my illness. *Tunisian*

An enemy does not become a friend until the ass becomes a doctor. *Medieval Arabic*

(*Note*   A Tunisian variant of this goes: 'An enemy does not become a friend until bran becomes flour.')

*See also*   Friends

## English, the

An Englishman is the Sultan's uncle on his mother's side. *Bedouin*

## Enjoyment

It is wise to enjoy yourself, but it is a virtue to create enjoyment. *Persian*

## Ennui

When time grows long it becomes a snake. *Maltese*

## Enterprise

Eat him for breakfast before he eats you for dinner. *Lebanese*

## Envy

Every eunuch scoffs at his master's prick. *Medieval Arabic*

Envy is a burden that no man knows how to put down. *Medieval Arabic*

Is not your neighbour's hen bigger than a goose? And is not his wife a maiden? *Turkish*

Eye of praise, eye of envy. *Tunisian*

The fathers have eaten sour grapes and set the children's teeth on edge. *Syrian*

## Equality

If I were a prince, and you were a prince, who would drive the asses? *Maltese*

## Evidence

There are feathers in your hair, O chicken thief. *Tunisian*

## Example

To teach the bride beat the cat. *Arabic*

## Excuses

As soon as she was tired of harvesting she said 'My sickle is dull'. *Arabic*

They asked the frog, 'Why don't you speak up?' The frog said, 'My mouth is full of water!' *Lebanese*

## Expectations

When they started to shoe the Sultan's horse, the beetle stretched out its leg. *Arabic*

Peaches do not grow on pear trees. *Maltese*

Hope without work is a tree without fruit. *Arabic*

The content of the pot is revealed by the spoon. *Arabic*

Dew never filled an empty well. *Algerian*

## Expediency

If the window lets in a draught, block it up with your clothes. *Lebanese*

Sell your new robes before you part with your old ones. *Moroccan*

## Experience

The first time even a duck dives in tail-first. *Turkish*

What is learned in youth is carved in stone. *Arabic*

The man who has scalded his lips on milk will blow on his ice-cream. *Turkish*

It is easy for a bachelor to divorce a woman. *Turkish*

One people's misfortunes are another people's instruction. *Lebanese*

It is not the cutting of the melon that cools the mouth. *Arabic*

He who is one day older than you is a year wiser. *Arabic*

He who falls in the river fears not the rain. *Omani*

# F

## Faculties

The mind is for seeing, the heart is for hearing. *Turkish*

Believe what you see and lay aside what you hear. *Arabic*

## Faith

When a man is satisfied he becomes an unbeliever.
*Arabic*

The mosque may be destroyed, but the mihrab remains.
*Turkish*

(*Note*  A mihrab is a prayer niche.)

Trust in God, but tie your camel. *Turkish*

The best rosary is the thread of a life hung with the
beads of love and thought. *Persian*

You can hope to be reconciled with any enemy except
your enemy in religion. *Arabic*

Unbelief is a single nation. *Tunisian*

My hunger is in my body, my satisfaction is in my soul.
*Tunisian*

Tilling is worship. *Arabic*

## Fame

If you wish to win reknown, commit an atrocity. *Arabic*

## Family

*See* Relatives

## Fantasies

He has no trousers, but his belt is forty cubits long.
*Moroccan*

## Farming

The well-to-do farmer is an acknowledged Sultan.
*Lebanese*

The man who plants corn sows holiness. *Persian*

## Fate

For every judge in Heaven there are two in Hell.
*Tunisian*

A thousand obstacles will meet you, even on-the way to
the grave. *Lebanese*

He who slaps his own face should not cry out. *Lebanese*

*See also* Destiny, Providence.

## Fatherhood

The man with no children has a hole in his heart; the man who has children has a heart like a sieve. *Tunisian*

If a man marries he embarks on a vessel; if he gets a child, he is wrecked. *Moroccan*

He who has children and livestock is always worried. *Maltese*

He who does not want his daughter to marry sets a high dowry. *South Lebanese*

No one knows when the man without daughters dies. *Moroccan*

When cares overwhelm you, take your son on your lap. *Egyptian*

When the son grows a beard, the father must shave his off. *Arabic*

When the father's trousers fit the son the father may as well step into the grave. *Maltese*

The children of the moustache will be raised by the beard, the children of the beard will be raised by white hair, and the children of white hair will be raised as orphans. *Arabic*

*See also* Parenthood, Relatives


## Fear

By night fear waits at the door, by day it runs in the hills. *Afghani*

Fear drives out pain. *Syrian*

When the lions are absent the jackals dance. *Arabic*

If we were afraid of sheep we would not wear wool.
*Moroccan*

## Fearlessness

When a man goes to a house knowing there is plague
in it he does not die a martyr. *Arabic*

## February

There are no rules in February. *Arabic*

February does not keep its word. *Lebanese*

February is the enemy of old women. *Lebanese*

## Fidelity

The fruit of fidelity grows on the palm of confidence.
*Arabic*

## Fire

Fire is the fruit of winter. *Syrian*

## Flattery

The letter written with musk should be sealed with
ambergris. *Medieval Arabic*

## Folly

He who takes a donkey up a minaret must bring it down. *Arabic*

There is no good in the man who ploughs his roof, and less good in the man who tries to help him. *Arabic*

At the age of sixty man's folly knows no limits. *Lebanese*

For an intelligent man to live with an idiot is a secret illness. *Arabic*

## Food

What is grass to the lion is flesh to the horse. *Turkish*

All roads lead to the mill. *Syrian*

Lunch and lie down, dine and take a walk. *Egyptian*

Ripe fruit carries its soul on its skin. *Maltese*

Roses are scented, but bread keeps us alive. *Maltese*

Work in the sun, eat in the shade. *Omani*

Eat onions wherever you find them. *Omani*

Eat as much garlic as you can get. *Omani*

If you must eat pig, make sure it's fat. *Moorish*

A man's bread is a debt he owes to others. *Lebanese*

If you can't get the meat, drink the gravy. *Arabic*

Those who dwell beside water have no worries about food. *Omani*

When food is served, conversation stops. *Iraqi*

Food for one is enough for two. *Tunisian*

Everyone with a mouth eats. *Arabic*

## Fools

Take from a fool, but give him nothing. *Saudi Arabian*

## Forethought

Before putting scissors to cloth a man should know what he wants to cut. *Maltese*

The wise man digs a well before he steals a minaret. *Arabic*

## Forgetfulness

When a man rides his horse he forgets about God, and when he dismounts he forgets about his horse. *Arabic*

## Forgiveness

Only when the fault is forgotten is forgiveness complete. *Arabic*

## Freedom

Better a stray dog than a caged lion. *Syrian*

The free man is a slave to his desires, but a slave is a free man when his desires are satisfied. *Medieval Arabic*

The potter attaches the handle to the jug on any side he pleases. *Lebanese*

Every monkey has its chain. *Syrian*

## Friends and friendship

He who is for you is for you, and he who is against you is against you. *Arabic*

No path is steep that leads to a friend. *Arabic*

From the hand of a friend a stone is an apple. *Arabic*

An old friend is like a ready saddled horse. *Afghani*

The man without a spoon will burn his hand. *Arabic*

Business comes in ounces, friendship comes in pounds. *Turkish*

Man will travel a mile to visit the sick, two miles to mend a quarrel, and three miles to see a friend. *Arabic*

Bring your hearts together, but keep your tents separate. *Arabic*

Beware of your enemy twice, but beware of your friend a thousand times. *Syrian*

Your real enemy is your best friend. *Maltese*

47

Seeing his friend being disembowelled, he asked 'Will you give me some for my cat?' *Lebanese*

Your brothers are those who bought you, not those who sold you. *Lebanese*

If your friend is honey, do not lick him all up. *Tunisian*

How many friends I had when my vines produced honey, how few now that they are withered. *Arabic*

To die among friends is a feast. *Arabic*

(*Note* A Tunisian variant of this very popular proverb goes 'To be hanged with friends is a picnic'.)

You know a man when you need him. *Maltese*

There are not two Gods in heaven, and no two people really love one another on earth. *Lebanese*

A drop of blood is worth a thousand friends. *Arabic*

There is no formality among friends. *Omani*

If you dress, dress in silk, and if you have a friend let him be a prince. *Arabic*

Better to be eaten by dogs than to be forced to seek help from friends. *Maltese*

A man who starts a quarrel without allies is like the man who goes to the well without ropes. *Sudanese*

Let me sever the cord of our friendship, so that when the ends are tied up again we will be even closer. *Persian*

## Frugality

An onion without cares is better than a chicken with troubles. *Lebanese*

## Future, the

The future is near. *Lebanese*

# G

## Gardening

Rose breeder, thorn's servant. *Turkish*

## Generosity

Generosity casts a long shadow. *Arabic*

Generosity veils all faults. *Arabic*

The tree with too many nests dies before the others.
*Algerian*

The root of evil is charity. *Lebanese*

Bread given to honourable men is a loan; bread given to
dishonourable men is alms. *Syrian*

If you have much, give of your wealth, if you have little
give of your heart. *Arabic*

The man who brings a gift on a donkey will receive one
on a camel. *Arabic*

*See also* Gifts

## Genius

The son of a genius is never a genius and if he were he
would surpass his father. *Lebanese*

## Ghouls

Ghouls enter by the open door. *Arabic*


## Gifts and giving

The hand that gives is higher than the hand that takes. *Turkish*

To give quickly is to give twice. *Turkish*

A gift is welcome, though it be but a bean. *Moorish*

If God gives you anything, take it! *Arabic*

Small gifts come from the heart, big gifts come from the purse. *Turkish*

He who gives you a rope will bind you with it. *Tunisian*

The man who gives you something has already taken something away from you. *Maltese*

Whatever I give remains mine. *Turkish*

What a child gives is what he no longer wants. *Arabic*

*See also* Generosity


## Girls

As soon as she can stand a girl searches out what is hidden. *Algerian*

Girls resemble their aunts. *Yemeni*

Better a pleasant ape than an unpleasant gazelle.
*Lebanese*

Better the wiles of a snake than the coquetry of a young girl. *Arabic*

Boys think of ships, girls think of the future. *Maltese*

After puberty, a husband or a grave. *Arabic*

A girl possesses nothing but a veil and a tomb. *Saudi Arabian*

It is a custom to kiss a girl in her father's house; it is a crime to kiss her in yours. *Kurdish*

Flowers break rocks. *Tunisian*


## Gluttony

Eating on a full stomach is like scooping out a grave with your own teeth. *Turkish*


## God

Knowledge is manifold, but the deity is one. *Arabic*

God is not seen. He is recognised by the mind. *Arabic*

That which is in God's mind is not in man's. *Lebanese*

God's belly is large. *Iraqi*

The bone of God is the calamity of Death. *Arabic*

God is greater than the Sultan. *Iraqi*

God waits forty years. *Iraqi*

The legs of the man who seeks a proof of God are made of wood. *Persian*

God does not take from the empty-handed. *Arabic*

Choose God, or choose dates, but you cannot choose both. *Persian*

God is more merciful than His creation. *Arabic*

If God did not forgive, Paradise would be empty. *Arabic*

God's cudgel strikes without sound and without remedy. *Persian*

For every door God closes He opens a thousand others. *Turkish*

God hears things in reverse. *Lebanese*

God makes shoes upside down. *Lebanese*

Sit on a wasp's nest and say 'God wills it!' *Lebanese*

God gives you one thing and takes away another. *Arabic*

God often intervenes between the fork and the mouth. *Arabic*


### Good and bad

The thorn engenders the rose and the rose engenders the thorn. *Arabic*

Rain was not created solely to make mud. *Moroccan*

Nakedness is from God, filth from the Devil. *Arabic*

## Gossip

He who gossips to you will gossip about you. *Algerian*

If you want to teach your child how to talk, apprentice him to a barber. *Tunisian*

The dirt that comes out of a hole will fill it up again. *Lebanese*

She who conceives in secret will give birth in public. *Arabic*

## Government

When an official appears, spit in his face. *Moorish*

*See also* Authority, Power

## Graffiti

Walls are fools' notebooks. *Lebanese*

## Gratitude

Thanks do not fill the belly. *Maltese*

No load is heavier than gratitude. *Turkish*

Even a hen acknowledges Heaven when she takes water. *Turkish*

The dog loves the man who strangles him. *Sudanese*

Give me wool today and tomorrow I will give you a sheep.
*Syrian*

*See also* Ingratitude

## Greed

Having too much is the same as having too little. *Arabic*

If a cat swims it is because he wants to steal something.
*Arabic*

As soon as they are told to save water everyone begins
to drink. *Arabic*

A wide eye and a narrow purse. *Arabic*

The beard of the greedy is up the arse of the bankrupt.
*Lebanese*

The ewe that went to get horns returned without ears.
*Omani*

No cat flees a wedding. *Moroccan*

## Grief

Grieve for the living, not for the dead. *Turkish*

The woman bereaved loves the woman bereaved.
*Medieval Arabic*

No one need teach the orphan how to grieve. *Arabic*

## Guesswork

An intelligent surmise is better than a stupid fact. *Arabic*

## Guests

Do not ask a guest questions until he has been entertained three days. *Bedouin*

The guest should veil his eyes, eat what is offered, and not gossip. *Arabic*

A new guest arrives and the whole neighbourhood plays host. *Egyptian*

Guests and fish stink after three days. *Bedouin*

The host is his guest's prisoner. *Arabic*

An unwelcome guest lingers like the British Empire. *Iraqi*

A guest is a guest, even if he stays all winter and summer. *Arabic*

Summer rain, the stars in the cold season, the word of a guest: there is no trusting any of them. *Moroccan*

## Guides

He who takes a cock for his guide will sleep in the henhouse. *South Lebanese*

*See also*  Travel

## Guilt

Repentance is no use. *Omani*

Even if guilt were made of sable no one would choose to wear it. *Turkish*

## Guns

The loaded gun terrifes one man; the unloaded gun terrifies two. *Persian*

# H

## Habits

Habits are worse than rabies. *Turkish*

Men from the same province make the same gestures. *Turkish*

Habit always triumphs. *Arabic*

Only the shroud can cure your habits. *Arabic*

Never buy from the same shop, never walk down the same street. *Maltese*

## Happiness

When God wants to make a poor man happy He makes him lose his ass and then find it again. *Turkish*

Happiness flies. *Arabic*

*See also* Contentment

## Hardship

One man sold his son because of need, another bought him on credit. *South Lebanese*

*See also* Misfortune, Poverty

## Harmony

Harmony should be sought even in the blast of a trumpet. *Turkish*

## Haste

Haste comes from the devil. *Arabic*

Only three things warrant haste: the marriage of a daughter, the burial of the dead, and the feeding of a guest. *Persian*

## Health

For the healthy man every day is a wedding. *Turkish*

Bid good day to the bean merchant, not the drug seller. *Arabic*

Health is the best feast. *Yemeni*

For every argument the liver loses a drop of blood. *Persian*

My health is more precious than my wealth, my anklets and my earrings. *Tunisian*

*See also* Illness, Medicine

## Heart, the

The heart is like a glass castle: it cannot be mended. *Turkish*

Like a child, the heart hopes for what it desires. *Turkish*

He who has no heart dies fat. *Arabic*

## Height

He who is tall eats figs, while he who is short dies of chagrin. *Lebanese*

## Help

Wait until your cart has overturned, then people will show you the way. *Turkish*

## Heredity

The man descended from dogs will bark. *Arabic*

Only a mule denies his origin. *Arabic*

A rose can come from a thorn, a thorn can come from a rose. *Arabic*

The hedgehog put her hand on her children and smiled: 'You are all prickly!' *Lebanese*

Young or old, the raven is beaked. *Arabic*

Only the tortoise looks just like his father. *Arabic*

No mould can straighten a dog's tail. *Turkish*

The white dog and the black dog are both sons of bitches. *Lebanese*

The scorpion is sister to the snake. *Arabic*

## Hire

The rented donkey always dies. *Arabic*

## History

Little by little the sea devours the shore. *Maltese*

## Home

Better black bread in your own house than honey at your neighbour's. *Arabic*

Rent before food. *Arabic*

It takes three children to make a home. *Kurdish*

Every dog barks at its own door. *Moroccan*

When your house falls in ruins, don't weep for the broken pots. *Arabic*

You can live in one house but not in ten. *Syrian*

In every house there is a drain. *Lebanese*

Every man is a child in his own home. *Arabic*

Better to live in a small cottage by yourself than in a palace with other people. *Maltese*

The guest is more honoured than your father. *Arabic*

A house without an elderly person is like an orchard without a well. *Arabic*

A house without children is like a garden without flowers. *Tunisian*

Your home hides your shame. *Arabic*

A house with one wife is prosperous; a house with two wives is a ruin; in a house with three wives – take down your trousers and defecate! *Lebanese*

Man makes the money, woman builds the home. *Arabic*

## Homo sapiens

God made man to lay up barley for asses. *Lebanese*

## Honesty

He who speaks the truth will lose his head. *Arabic*

Nudes only suit each other in the bath. *Turkish*

*See also* Truth

## Honour

Honour lies in the mane of a horse. *Arabic*

(*Note* In this proverb possession of a mount signifies a worthy social position.)

Bedding, manure heaps and honour must all be straightened quickly. *Arabic*

It is better to change one's mind a thousand times than to be cheated once. *Lebanese*

## Horses

Care for your horse as though he were a friend; ride your horse as though he were an enemy. *Turkish*

The back of a horse is a fan. *South Lebanese*

## Hospitality

The house that receives no guests receives no angels. *Arabic*

A stranger's hospitality is always on loan. *Afghani*

(*Note*  In other words, it must be returned.)

If you accept the wolf's invitation, take a dog. *Turkish*

A kind welcome is better than a good dinner. *Egyptian*

There is no compassion in the house where they don't give you something to smoke. *Syrian*

*See also*  Guests

## Houses

The best houses have wide courtyards, high ceilings, tall entrances, and distant toilets. *Lebanese*

If you wish to squander your money, buy an old house and restore it. *Iraqi*

The pleasure of food and drink lasts an hour, of sleep a day, of women a month, but of a building a lifetime. *Arabic*

The house of a tyrant is a ruin. *Omani*

A woman's house is her tomb. *Arabic*

In building is despair. *Lebanese*

## Human nature

Beware! You know he is human! *Maltese*

To put your trust in men is like putting water in a sieve. *Arabic*

Even a man's own entrails quarrel with one another. *Lebanese*

He who is born round will not die square. *Maltese*

The world belonged to two men: one was killed by the other. *Lebanese*

One man donates oil to the lamps of the mosque, the next man steals it. *Saudi Arabian*

Cropping a donkey's ears will not produce a stallion. *Turkish*

Every wood burns quietly except the thorn: the thorn cries 'I am wood as well!' *Persian*

Wash a dog and it will be even dirtier. *Lebanese*

The man without a witness is a liar. *Tunisian*

Every generation curses its predecessor. *Arabic*

Everyone is good, but that's no reason to trust them. *Maltese*

A dog is a dog, even the one with a golden collar. *Arabic*

*See also* Character types, Men, Women

## Humility

The head that is bowed will not be cut off. *Turkish*

Humility is a net to ensnare the high-ranking. *Medieval Arabic*

Humility is the crown of manhood. *Medieval Arabic*

*See also* Pride

## Hunger

The hungry stomach has no ears. *Turkish*

Fast for a year and feast on a rotten locust. *Tunisian*

*See also* Poverty

## Hypocrisy

The judge's servant dies and everyone attends the funeral; the judge dies, and no one attends the funeral. *Moroccan*

Everyone has rubbish in front of his own house. *Omani*

# I

## Idleness

The busy are tempted by the Devil, but the Devil is tempted by idleness. *Turkish*

## Ignorance

When one blind man leads another, both fall into a hole. *Arabic*

Ignorance is an incurable disease. *Saudi Arabian*

To be without books is to be like a Dalmatian. *Turkish*

No empty sack can stand up straight. *Turkish*

The ignorant man is a soldier without weapons. *Arabic*

The ignorant man always covers the same ground twice. *Medieval Arabic*

What does a donkey know about ginger? *Moroccan*

Man is the enemy of what he doesn't know. *Arabic*

Blind in this world, blind in the next. *Koranic*

## Illness

Cold and poverty cause every illness. *Arabic*

God is the only doctor. *Arabic*

God created the disease and God created the cure. *Arabic*

Patience mends the broken bone. *Tunisian*

All invalids are cruel. *Lebanese*

An enemy's visit to the sickbed is worse than the disease itself. *Arabic*

The woman who sleeps with a blind man will wake up cross-eyed. *Turkish*

## Imagination

He who sits on the bank of the river is always a great swimmer. *Moorish*

The locust flies with the wings of a falcon. *Saudi Arabian*

## Immigrants

Scattered grain attracts birds from Tunis to Taza. *Moroccan*

## Impatience

An egg today, no chicken tomorrow. *Arabic*

The wise man pauses, the fool crosses the stream. *Turkish*

To ask the price of a fish before it has been caught. *Arabic*

## Impoliteness

A fart never shattered any flagstones. *Lebanese*

## Impossibilities

You can't fry an egg in the wind. *Lebanese*

You can't break a stone with an egg. *Lebanese*

## Imprisonment

The longest sentences should be reserved for the tongue.
*Arabic*

## Impudence

An impudent face will not die wrinkled. *Maltese*

Who should tell the lion it has bad breath? *Tunisian*

He who demands morning from God will be blind when
the sun rises. *Arabic*

## Inactivity

Water left in a jar soon goes bad. *Arabic*

If he is idle, buy him a camel! *Arabic*

*See also* Idleness

## Incompetence

He who does not know how to dance says the floor is uneven. *Egyptian*

## Inconsistence

Like a rabbit, one year male, one year female. *Arabic*

## Increase

The man without a bull from his cow or a boy from his wife may as well be dead. *Tunisian*

## Indebtedness

Even mullahs have to borrow. *Yemeni*

Life is borrowing and paying back. *Lebanese*

## Individuality

Every man is the master of his own beard. *Arabic*

## Indulgence

The man who touches honey must lick his fingers. *Arabic*

## Inevitability

What comes down must rise up. *Syrian*

## Inflation

The cure for high prices is abstinence. *Tunisian*

## Inflexibility

Winter is over, but still the charcoal man's face is black.
*Persian*

## Information

How much news purchased today will be free tomorrow?
*Egyptian*

*See also* News

## Ingratitude

Give a man some cloth and he'll ask for some lining.
*Turkish*

Beware of the man to whom you have done a good turn.
*Lebanese*

Call someone your lord and he'll sell you in the slave
market. *Arabic*

The well-fed dog savages its owner. *Lebanese*

I taught him to swim and he drowned me. *Moorish*

I put a date in his mouth and he poked me in the eye
with a stick. *Tunisian*

He took the bait and shat on the hook. *Lebanese*

*See also* Gratitude

70

## Inhumanity

Should my beard catch fire others will use it to light their pipes. *Turkish*

## Injunctions

Do not chase the wind that carries off your hat. *Kurdish*

Do not lick what you have spat. *Turkish*

Have no pity for the child raised in a kitchen, or for the guardian of a vineyard. *Yemeni*

Think much, speak little, write less. *Maltese*

Tell the truth and give away your surplus. *Koranic*

Drink like a camel and rise up early. *Lebanese*

Insert your brains inside your head. *Lebanese*

Eat the present, then break the dish. *Arabic*

(*Note* I.e. avoid obligations)

Veil your women and repair your ramparts. *Algerian*

## Insanity

Insanity is manifold: it has seventy gates. *Lebanese*

A country without an asylum for the insane is empty. *Tunisian*

In this world the insane far outnumber the sane. *Maltese*

To gain respect act insane. *Moroccan*

Every day is a holiday for the madman. *Turkish*

## Insignificance

No caravan stops for the bark of a dog. *Turkish*

## Insincerity

Many are the roads that do not lead to the heart. *Arabic*

Fear not the man who smiles, but fear the man who pats your back. *Maltese*

The victim murdered, the funeral attended. *Egyptian*

## Insolence

Every insolent man has wounds. *Turkish*

## Insults

The wound of words is worse than the wound of swords. *Arabic*

## Intelligence

Everyone is perfectly satisfied with his own intelligence. *Arabic*

Only intelligence becomes more precious as it becomes more plentiful. *Lebanese*

## Intentions

If a man wishes you well, burn your furniture to heat his pot. *Persian*

## Interference

Those who don't hunt shouldn't scare the game. *Arabic*

## Intrusion

The uninvited guest must sit on the floor. *Turkish*

## Iraq

The Yemen is a cradle to the Arabs, Iraq their grave. *Arabic*

# J

## Jealousy

He who is not jealous is an ass. *Lebanese*

## Justice

Justice is good, but no one wants it in his own house.
*Maltese*

The man who is just by night will have a house by day.
*Arabic*

When a ruler is just everyone is in his army. *Persian*

He who eats the eggs of a judge must give back
chickens. *Arabic*

The favour of the judge is worth two witnesses. *Lebanese*

*See also* Law

# K

## Kindness

Kindness to slaves silences the ill-natured. *Arabic*

The gentle heart does not grow old. *Tunisian*

## Knowledge

More precious than the blood of a martyr is the ink of knowledge. *Arabic*

A well-stocked brain is the sign of a generous mind. *Bedouin*

It is better to know things than not to know things. *Moroccan*

No man has enough knowledge. *Arabic*

As knowledge increases men grow more evil. *Maltese*

He who knows nothing is well off. *Maltese*

Seek knowledge, even though it be in China. *Arabic*

*See also* Learning, Wisdom

# L

## Labour

The saw is wealth, the axe is waste. *Maltese*

## Ladders

Stairs are safer than ladders. *Arabic*

## Landlords

No one rules you except the man who can say 'Give me money or get out of your house!' *Arabic*

## Languages

Every language requires a people. *Arabic*

## Law, the

The man who goes to court feeds on sardines while his lawyer dines on woodcock. *Maltese*

O God, grant our judge considerable legal wealth!
*Lebanese*

When the judge is against you avoid his courthouse.
*Arabic*

It is the man with little honour who becomes a judge.
*Lebanese*

The gallows are for the poor. *Maltese*

*See also* Justice

## Laziness

If an egg had two handles it would take two men to carry it. *Egyptian*

The winds blow, yet the ships are becalmed. *Medieval Arabic*

## Leadership

In calm weather everyone is captain. *Maltese*

If you wish to destroy a country, pray that it has many chiefs. *Lebanese*

By you she will flower, by you she will wither. *Arabic*

When the leader dies the nation's fire is put out. *Arabic*

When the shepherd is corrupt, so is his flock. *Moorish*

## Learning

A scholar who does not produce is like a cloud that doesn't rain. *Arabic*

If all your learning comes from books, you are more often wrong than right. *Lebanese*

Practice shaving on madmen. *Omani*

*See also*   Education, Knowledge, Wisdom

## Leisure

The man who takes up fishing is destroyed. *Maltese*

## Letters

Letters written after dinner are read in Hell. *Turkish*

## Lies and liars

Words have their use, lies add ornament. *Persian*

Lies are wings. *Afghani*

When a man hears his own lie at the far end of the market he believes it. *Turkish*

The mother of the liar is a virgin. *Medieval Arabic*

A liar's candle keeps burning until the first watch. *Turkish*

Lying lets you live one night, the truth makes you live forever. *Tunisian*

Like a sword without a hilt the lie cuts the hand that grips it. *Arabic*

Truth builds, lies destroy. *Arabic*

A good liar needs a good memory. *Arabic*

You may lunch on lies, but you cannot dine on them as well. *Yemeni*

Follow the liar to the door of his house. *Moorish*

## Life

The world is a pot, and man is its ladle. *Turkish*

Life begins in smoke and ends in ashes. *Arabic*

Life is the quarantine for Paradise. *Arabic*

What is past is a dream, what is to come is a desire. *Arabic*

The whole world is nothing but the scraping of a donkey. *Arabic*

The world shows you the mare and gives you the ass. *Maltese*

The man who is not dead still has a chance. *Lebanese*

Life is a peep-show. *Arabic*

The date palm has its feet in water and its head in fire. *Arabic*

When one's fate comes, the eye is blind. *Arabic*

It is ten thousand times better to live in distress than sleep under a stone. *Lebanese*

One day honey, one day onions. *Sudanese*

Is there anything more than death? *Lebanese*

At the close of night the wailing begins. *Arabic*

## Lifestyles

Better the sword than the Indian hemp. *Moroccan*

## Listening

Listening requires more intelligence than speaking.
*Turkish*

The ear does not increase in size according to what it
hears. *Iraqi*

*See also* Speech

## Loneliness

To die with others is better than living alone. *Moorish*

## Longevity

Three things prolong life: a big house, a swift horse, and
an obedient wife. *Arabic*

## Loose living

A span of debauchery rather than a cubit of cloth.
*Lebanese*

## Love

Love and blindness are companions. *Arabic*

Love is an outrage. *Egyptian*

For the lover, Baghdad is next door. *Turkish*

Love veils defects. *Syrian*

For seven seconds love; for seven minutes fantasy; for the rest of your life misery. *Arabic*

When love comes, manners go. *Tunisian*

The blow of a loved one is an apple. *Arabic*

(*Note*   A Syrian version of this one runs: 'The blow of a loved one is a raisin, the stone he throws a pomegranate.')

He who would be loved must begin by loving. *Arabic*

An onion offered with love is worth a sheep. *Egyptian*

Time fastens friendships, love unravels them. *Persian*

The essence of love is Take! *Sudanese*

Everyone in love is the same. *Moroccan*

People hate the man who loves himself. *Arabic*

One thread for the needle, one love for the heart. *Sudanese*

*See also*   Male and female


## Loyalty

Memory is a falcon that cannot be held; loyalty is a sparrow's nest which cannot be repaired. *Turkish*

## Luck

Good luck comes to him who has it, not to him who seeks it. *Arabic*

With good luck the dove lays eggs on a peg; with bad luck the donkey pisses on the lion. *Lebanese*

The unlucky find bones even in a liver. *Lebanese*

The unlucky chick trips over in the egg. *Moorish*

The unlucky mouse sees the cheese but not the cat. *Arabic*

Drop the lucky man in the Nile and he surfaces with a fish in his mouth. *Arabic*

Start selling turbans and people are born without heads. *Arabic*

What the winds bring the gales remove. *Lebanese*

No stone worthy of a wall will be found on a road. *Persian*

Come the gallows and the devil bids adieu. *Turkish*


## Lust

Two hungry lovers and a single bed signifies the birth of a beggar. *Turkish*

# M

## Male and female

A woman is a cane, a man is nerves. *Yemeni*

Man is a river, woman is a lake. *Kurdish*

The man reaps, the woman builds. *Lebanese*

A man laughs with his heart, a woman laughs with her mouth. *Arabic*

A man's heart is like a cabbage: he gives it away leaf by leaf but retains the centre for his wife. *Maltese*

Two bull camels cannot share one herd. *Moroccan*

The beauty of a man is in his intelligence: the intelligence of a woman is in her beauty. *Arabic*

Lecherous men are only conquered by lecherous women, and lecherous women are only conquered by the grave. *Arabic*

Better an ape that makes you laugh than a gazelle that makes you weep. *Sudanese*

A kiss without love cuts off the moustaches. *Tunisian*

It is easier for a sieve to hold water than for a woman to trust a man. *Lebanese*

If a woman loves a man she will give it to him even through a hole in the door. *Moroccan*

Four women in the tent means an empty water-skin. *Algerian*

*See also*  Love, Marriage, Men, Women


## Maltese

Do not rent a two-storey house to a Maltese, for he will spit on your head. *Maltese*


## Manners

The man who farts conquers the man scented with frankincense. *Lebanese*


## Markets

Markets are God's repasts served on earth. *Arabic*


## Marriage

Marriage is like a castle under siege: those within want to get out, those outside want to get in. *Arabic*

Something goes wrong at every wedding. *Arabic*

A wedding without gifts is like a corpse without perfumes. *Lebanese*

Accompany a funeral procession, but stay away from weddings. *Syrian*

The tongue is moist when it asks in marriage, but afterwards it dries up like wood. *Omani*

You have to spend a lot of money to get a bride. *Lebanese*

If you don't know what your betrothed looks like, examine the face of her brother. *Arabic*

Rather than remain in her parents' house a woman should take a husband of wood. *Arabic*

As long as the bride-dresser eats her fill, the rest of the party may go hungry. *Yemeni*

The fool praises his wife, the wise man praises his dog. *Turkish*

However many times she has been passed over, marry the woman of noble birth. *Arabic*

Choose your horse with the eyes of a young man, but choose your wife with the eyes of an old man. *Arabic*

The best marriage is the one that doesn't take place. *Maltese*

The woman who marries the man who loves her will do better than the woman who marries the man she loves. *Arabic*

The bridegroom is a prince for seven days, for seven days a vizier, and for the rest of his life a prisoner. *Tunisian*

Never marry a foolish woman, even if her cheeks are of musk. *Persian*

When an old man takes a young wife the youth of the town rejoice. *Moorish*

85

When the amber-cutter takes a wife she will wear pearls of glass. *Persian*

If you are not already mad when you marry, you will be when you realise you have to swing the cradle. *Maltese*

The man who is shy of his wife will have no children. *Lebanese*

The blind husband must eat what his mad wife cooks. *Lebanese*

Better a neat bed than a messy husband. *Moroccan*

He who cannot control his mother-in-law takes vengeance on his wife. *Lebanese*

Listen to what your wife says, but do as you please. *Maltese*

Widows and young girls, have pity for wives! *Arabic*

Lucky is the woman who has daughters before sons. *Lebanese*

A well-matched marriage is Hell on earth; an ill-matched marriage is hard labour. *Maltese*

I told her 'I divorce you!' She said 'Come to bed!' *Iraqi*

The best part of marriage takes place before the wedding. *Arabic*

What may a man not endure, except the mention of his wives? *Persian*

A short woman always looks young to her husband. *Arabic*

Don't reveal your secret to your husband, lest he tire of you. *Tunisian*

A co-wife is a co-wife, even if she is the handle of a jar. *Arabic*

There is no pain like tooth-ache, no trouble like marriage. *Tunisian*

Better the blows of a sledgehammer than a wife's complaints in bed. *Lebanese*

She dies noble who guards the purse and drives out the enemy. *Arabic*

When you see your wife blowing her nose with her veil, divorce her. *Moorish*

There is no separation in Christian marriage except by strangulation. *Lebanese*

A second wife is a bitter thing. *Lebanese*

Every man with two wives is a porter. *Kurdish*

Do not marry your lover, and do not take back the man you have divorced. *Arabic*

The wife whose husband is away dines on couscous with chicken. *Tunisian*

When a woman is accompanied by her husband she can spin the moon on her finger. *Syrian*

Be good to your own wife and you can have your neighbour's. *Arabic*

The death of the wife is the renewal of the wedding. *Egyptian*

See also   Love, Male and female, Men, Remarriage, Women

## Meanness

You who are stingy with the meat will be sorry when you see the soup. *Arabic*

## Means and ends

To pull out a rusty nail it may be necessary to pull down the whole wall. *Arabic*

When there are no horses, saddle the dogs. *Arabic*

Why burn the blanket to destroy the flea? *Turkish*

One stone is sufficient to frighten a thousand crows. *Turkish*

Green wood will burn if there is enough dry wood with it. *Turkish*

Wear what covers, eat what there is. *Tunisian*

Either the bread is dry, or the knife is dull. *Maltese*

A running stream is better than a dry river. *Arabic*

You can't make a drum from a ratskin. *Omani*

Big bulls make crooked furrows. *Syrian*

A live ass is better than a dead philosopher. *Lebanese*

Only the hounds of Mazandaran can catch the jackals of Mazandaran. *Persian*

(*Note* Mazandaran is a province in the north of Iran, lying on the Caspian Sea.)

*See also* Consequences

## Medicine

Nature offers a balm for every sore. *Bedouin*

The man who conceals his pain will never find a cure. *Turkish*

A scorpion in the sleeve, the doctor in Bagdad. *Arabic*

He who comes to cure the eye will put it out. *Moroccan*

Fate can make a fool of any physician. *Arabic*

*See also* Illness

## Memory

Do good and forget it; do evil, and you will remember. *Maltese*

*See also* Loyalty

## Men

Man is a bird without wings. *Syrian*

Anything is better than man. *Lebanese*

It takes four days to learn about an animal, but only two days to learn about a man. *Persian*

After God created man God repented. *Moroccan*

Be kind to dogs, not men. *Lebanese*

There is no good in a man who cannot read his letters, slaughter his sheep, wash his hair or cook his dinner. *Moroccan*

A gentleman is gentle. *Arabic*

Nine out of ten men are women. *Turkish*

He who echoes your words like the vault of a bath is not a man. *Turkish*

Walls are cast down by damp, men are cast down by troubles. *Turkish*

Man hides behind his teeth. *Arabic*

(*Note*  An equally common proverb is: 'Man hides beneath his tongue.')

The heart only reveals itself in battle, and the head only reveals itself on the road. *Arabic*

Expect no good from a man who is not ashamed of men. *Arabic*

Women ask questions, men give the answers. *Moorish*

Male camels give neither silk nor wool. *Moorish*

The worst of men is he who eats alone, refuses aid and beats his slave. *Arabic*

The man whose finger is in the water is not the man whose finger is in the fire. *Lebanese*

Every man's madness is different. *Lebanese*

Two weak men get the better of one strong man. *Arabic*

Every tall man is an idiot, every short man sows sedition. *Lebanese*

Women have two tricks, men have one. *Arabic*

Entering manhood is easy; getting out is not so easy. *Moorish*

The old man dies to get what the young man desires. *Arabic*

*See also*   Male and female, Women

## Miserliness

A rich man who is ungenerous is like a tree without fruit. *Arabic*

Every miser wants a wooden cat. *Lebanese*

(*Note*   I.e. to hunt mice, but which won't eat anything.)

If you love meat, slaughter your camel. *Tunisian*

## Misfortune

Life's misfortunes are more numerous than plants. *Arabic*

For every grape a hundred wasps. *Persian*

Like a bar of soap, a misfortune begins as something large, but becomes something small. *Arabic*

## Misogyny

The man who hates women hates his mother. *Maltese*

## Mockery

He who mocks dances without a tambourine. *Arabic*

## Modern times

The old days with their generous men are gone; nowadays the times carry an axe and whoever speaks the truth will get it in the neck. *Medieval Arabic*

## Modesty

Anyone can climb on the back of a small horse. *Turkish*

## Money

Money is the dust in the house of the world. *Arabic*

Money cleaves a path in the sea. *Arabic*

Money summons the most obstinate djinn. *Yemeni*

Money gives life to the soul, cleanses the filthy, and makes the old man a bridegroom. *Tunisian*

Stolen money walks in the darkness. *Arabic*

There is no messenger like money. *Arabic*

In this world everything passes except false money. *Maltese*

Money strays, but men bring it home. *Tunisian*

The value of money is having it. *Lebanese*

Kill the man who steals your money. *Arabic*

The money of the Christians is spent in opposition and rivalry; the money of the Jews is spent on religious festivities; the money of the Moslems is spent on pilgrimage and Holy War. *Moroccan*

Dirhams have sown discord among Moslems. *Medieval Arabic*

Do not count the days of the month in which you have no wages. *Arabic*

Keep your white money for the sad years. *Turkish*

*See also*   Wealth

## Mortality

The eye of man can only be filled with a handful of dust. *Arabic*

*See also*   Transience

## Motherhood

No grief is greater than a mother's. *Maltese*

She who conceives on the oven will give birth on the threshing floor. *Egyptian*

Every pig is beautiful in the eyes of its mother. *Moroccar*

Do not rejoice, mother of ten; do not be sad, mother of one. *Tunisian*

The mother of the mute understands what he says. *Arabic*

The mother of the victim never forgets; the mother of the assassin does not remember. *Lebanese*

The mother of a murdered man sleeps; the mother of an imprisoned man does not. *Lebanese*

The kind-hearted mother dies unhappy. *Arabic*

*See also*   Fatherhood, Parenthood, Relatives


## Mountains

What does one mountain know about another mountain's anger? *Turkish*


## Muscat

We who have seen Muscat and its customs houses are not amazed at the sight of a donkey dragging its girth. *Omani*

(*Note*   Muscat is the capital, and formerly chief port, of the Sultanate of Oman.)

# N

## Nationality

By country my brother, by religion my enemy. *Arabic*

## Nature

A bird in the wild is never free from care. *Arabic*

The wild ass needs no vet. *Moorish*

Better a mountain goat than a city philosopher. *Lebanese*

Honour the date palm, for it is your aunt. *Arabic*

Ears grow first, but horns grow longest. *Turkish*

The snake is thirsty and the innocent frog suffers.
*Moroccan*

The clouds are not harmed by the barking of dogs.
*Syrian*

If there were any good in the owl, the hawk would eat
him. *Tunisian*

There are no sweet onions, and there are no white pigs.
*Turkish*

The pumpkin's progeny spells trouble for the fence.
*Moroccan*

The sun warms but does not boil the pot. *Maltese*

## Need

If in need, go to a big house, for even if you get nothing to eat you can still sleep out of the cold. *Arabic*

He who has only wheat must borrow flour. *Moorish*

The donkey prefers a single thistle to an ass-load of jewels. *Persian*

It is a needy man who shears his dog. *Medieval Arabic*


## Neighbours

Good morning, Neighbour! You stay in your house, and I'll stay in mine! *Arabic*

He who counts on dinner with his neighbour goes to bed hungry. *Moroccan*

Love your neighbour, but don't let him in your house. *Maltese*

Better to quarrel with your mother than to quarrel with your neighbour. *Arabic*

A country where the stones know you is preferable to a country where the people know you. *Arabic*

Distance from people is great booty. *Arabic*


## News

When the rich man is pricked by a thorn the whole city knows; when the poor man is bitten by a snake the event is unrecorded. *Lebanese*

96

When the messenger is slow, the news is good. *Moorish*

Do not buy either the moon or the news, for in the end they will both come out. *Syrian*

## Night

Night is a pregnancy. *Turkish*

Night bears dark children. *Arabic*

## Nobility

The hand of the noble man is a balance. *Syrian*

A noble man cannot be harmed by manual labour. *Algerian*

# O

## Oaths

Everyone who swears is a liar. *Arabic*

## Obligation

He who eats the bread of the Sultan must strike with his sword. *Arabic*

## Occupation

The wife who makes lace has no time to fight duels over her husband's infidelities. *Maltese*

## Old age

Every old person acquires two faults: false hope and parsimony. *Arabic*

Like an onion, the heart is green, the head is white. *Arabic*

If you do not have an old man in the house, buy one. *Arabic*

A woman flees from old age as the ewe flees from the wolf. *Arabic*

During a famine the old have teeth. *Arabic*

An old bear is the plaything of his cubs. *Kurdish*

God shows no mercy on the man who loves the old. *Arabic*

When the falcon grows old the sparrows make a mock of him. *Arabic*

When the wolf gets old, the dogs laugh at him. *Arabic*

*See also* Transience.

## Omens

Take good omens from the mouths of children. *Arabic*

False news is a good omen. *Lebanese*

When the eyes roll in their orbits there is a devil in the stomach. *Arabic*

Winds in March, bad harvests in April. *Arabic*

An April shower is a jewel without price. *Arabic*

Not every cloud sheds rain. *Iraqi*

In a bad year the she-goat mounts the he-goat. *Lebanese*

When it thunders farts it will rain shit. *Lebanese*

White teeth, black heart. *Arabic*

When the lights of Canopus shine, touch dates in the night. *Arabic*

(*Note* Canopus (Alpha Carinae) is in the constellation Carina, and is the second brightest star in the night sky.)

It is an ill-fated woman who gives birth twice in one year. *Afghani*

It is not because the cock crows that the dawn breaks. *Arabic*

Too many cocks spoil the night. *Arabic*

## Opportunism

If a good thing comes your way, seize it. *Arabic*

To you the honour, to me the profit. *Kurdish*

When the times don't suit you, make sure you suit the times. *Turkish*

If the captain of the ship loves you, you may wipe your hands on the ship's sails. *Arabic*

The man with a free passage is sure to make a pass at the captain's wife. *Medieval Arabic*

When the lions depart, the jackals gather. *Arabic*

When the cow stumbles, many knives come out. *Arabic*

The right answer at the right time is worth an orchard and its fruit. *Lebanese*

Take from death before death takes from you. *Arabic*

Opportunities pass like clouds. *Syrian*

When one door closes, a hundred others open. *Arabic*

## Orphans

If you meet an orphan, throw him to the ground, for what right have you to be more compassionate than your Lord? *Tunisian*

On the heads of orphans hairdressers learn their trade. *Moroccan*

Orphaned of his mother, the child has the threshold as his pillow; orphaned of his father, he still has his mother's lap. *Tunisian*

# P

## Paradise

The key to Paradise is patience. *Turkish*

How far is it between me and Paradise? Lift up your head and look. *Arabic*

## Parasites

The man accustomed to dining at your table is always hungry. *Arabic*

Thanks to roses the thistles are irrigated. *Arabic*

## Parenthood

Children are a staircase to Paradise. *Persian*

Love your children but never show it. *Arabic*

Better a house full of men than a house full of wealth. *Moroccan*

The foolishness of someone else's child is always a joy. *Arabic*

Your fate is in the hands of your children. *Arabic*

The bed-bug has a hundred children and says 'How few!' *Arabic*

The child who is one night old has already learned how to annoy its parents. *Arabic*

He who cannot harden his heart cannot bring up children. *Arabic*

Raising children is like cracking flint with your teeth. *Lebanese*

When blind parents have a child they put its eyes out. *Lebanese*

The dung-beetle, seeing its child on the wall, thinks it sees a pearl on a thread. *Arabic*

My heart is for my child, but my child's heart is of stone. *Arabic*

There is no light in the eyes of a childless man. *Persian*

Blessings from your sister's children, happiness from your own. *Egyptian*

A man should correct his own son, but not his daughter's son, just as he should build on his own land and not on someone else's. *Egyptian*

To have children is a misfortune, and not to have children is a misfortune. *Arabic*

Parental love? – Pure chance! *Tunisian*

*See also* Fatherhood, Motherhood


## Patience

The man who can save his dinner for breakfast is bound to do well. *Arabic*

There is good in every delay. *Moroccan*

If meat is dear, patience is cheap. *Arabic*

Eat soup until God brings you meat. *Tunisian*

Fruit does not ripen at the touch of fingers. *Arabic*

The patience of the louse goes unnoticed. *Arabic*

Patience upon patience, until the grave. *Arabic*

No crowd ever waited at the gates of patience. *Moroccan*

It is with patience that the elephant succeeds in fucking the ant. *Maltese*

## Peasants

Never befriend a peasant, for unless he is oppressed he will oppress you. *Arabic*

If a peasant were made of silver his balls would be made of brass. *Lebanese*

## Perfection

The real defects of a thing only appear when it is finished. *Arabic*

## People

A man is most safe when most alone. *Arabic*

## Perseverence

The world is on the side of the man left standing. *Arabic*

Every beseiged city eventually falls. *Omani*

Hold on to the dog's tail until you have crossed the river. *Arabic*

Forty years I waited before the doors of Paradise, then as I slept they opened and shut. *Persian*

*See also* Resolution

## Persian

Flatter in Arabic, reprove in Turkish, but argue in Persian. *Persian*

## Personal conduct

Treat your superior as a father, your equal as a brother, and your inferior as a son. *Persian*

If you are an anvil be patient, but if you are a hammer, strike! *Arabic*

If you are sugar you will be swallowed, if you are wormwood you will be spat out. *Persian*

Sit awry but speak straight. *Arabic*

## Personal reform

Shit never turns to cream. *Lebanese*

## Piety

If you sin, hide it. *Arabic*

Hunger causes impiety. *Arabic*

Fear him who does not fear God. *Arabic*

There is no doorkeeper at the gate of Paradise. *Moroccan*

The slaughtered sheep does not suffer when one removes its skin. *Arabic*

## Plumpness

Show me rotundity and I will show you beauty. *Arabic*

Plumpness redeems the seven deadly sins. *Lebanese*

## Police

Obey them and cheat them. Whom? The police. *Maltese*

## Politics

It is better to herd cattle than rule men. *Arabic*

There is no religion in politics. *Lebanese*

A man who takes up politics is a man trying to climb into the garbage can. *Lebanese*

When the Sheikh dies his alliances die with him. *Arabic*

## Possessions

The best of your possessions is that which has profited you. *Arabic*

A dog's fleas are its jewels. *Maltese*

You hold on to your chickens, we will hold on to our cocks. *Tunisian*

One should never lend either one's wife or one's razor. *Maltese*

A bird in the hand is worth two on the wing. *Arabic*

## Position

Spit upwards and it lands on our moustache, spit downwards and it lands on our beard. *Arabic*

(*Note* Another version of this runs: 'Unable to speak up because of the moustache, unable to speak down because of the beard.')

The barking of a dog does not disturb the man on a camel. *Arabic*

It is better to be a garbage collector in the city than a Sultan in a village. *Lebanese*

## Poverty

Poverty is glorious to those worthy of it. *Koranic*

Poverty makes the heart blind. *Arabic*

Money begets money, lice beget lice. *Arabic*

Poverty is the shackle of clever men. *Syrian*

He who has no honey in his house should supply it with his tongue. *Moroccan*

The poor man's jaw aches with the rich man's wealth.
*Turkish*

It is better to itch all over than endure the worries of poverty. *Turkish*

God makes man feel the cold according to the state of his garments. *Arabic*

The sun is the cloak of the poor. *Arabic*

Before the rich man gives the poor man dies. *Turkish*

The rich man in a strange land is at home; the poor man at home is a stranger. *Arabic*

It is better to die in surfeit than live with an empty stomach. *Turkish*

The efforts of the poor are tears. *Arabic*

A poor woman is pregnant – good news for the graveyard. *Lebanese*

Poorer than a mosque mouse. *Arabic*

A thousand sparrows do not fill the pot. *Iraqi*

The roof always falls in on the heads of the poor. *Omani*

He is a porcupine castrator, didn't you know? *Lebanese*

(*Note* Said of someone without visible means of support.)

Poverty is wisdom. *Arabic*

*See also* Wealth

## Power

Every ruler sleeps on an ant-hill. *Afghani*

One lie in the Sultan's head provides an obstacle for twenty truths. *Arabic*

No bread, no power. *Turkish*

The bull protects his nose with his horns. *Arabic*

A lion's den never lacks bones. *Arabic*

When a great man becomes a bridge, take the long way round. *Kurdish*

To every Pharaoh a Moses. *Turkish*

There may be a thousand friends in the lair of the wolf. *Egyptian*

Beware the weapons of the weak. *Medieval Arabic*

(*Note*  This proverb was most commonly used to refer to prayers.)

*See also*  Authority

## Prayer

Sands will blow in the face of every man who prays. *Arabic*

Do not ask God to cut down the tree whose shade protects you. *Lebanese*

All the camels are fighting except ours, which is quietly kneeling. *Lebanese*

## Praise

To praise the unworthy is like saddling an ass with silk.
*Kurdish*

## Preachers

However large the congregation, the preacher preaches
as he pleases. *Turkish*

## Precautions

When they call you a reaper, sharpen your scythe. *Arabic*

It is on dark nights that people should count their apples.
*Afghani*

Before going in think about getting out. *Arabic*

*See also* Prudence

## Preferences

A sparrow in the mouth is better than a goose in the
sleeve. *Arabic*

Better a handful of bees than a basketful of flies.
*Moroccan*

A lively devil is better than a frigid angel. *Lebanese*

Smoke that blinds rather than cold that makes me ill.
*Syrian*

A bad camel is better than a good field. *Arabic*

(*Note* But another proverb has 'A bad field is better than a good camel'.)

## Prevention

Cut the cat's head off before it leaps. *Arabic*

## Pride

He who is proud has an enemy in God. *Turkish*

It is easier to spot an ant on black earth in the middle of the night than it is for a man to recognise his own pride. *Persian*

There is a pair of scissors for every moustache. *Omani*

He thinks he is ten measures of wheat done up in an embroidered sack. *Arabic*

The rich man takes pride in his purse, the scholar in his pamphlets. *Arabic*

There are three things one should never feel ashamed of: service at home, service to a guest, and service to one's mount. *Arabic*

Better to live one afternoon as a cock than six days as a chicken. *Tunisian*

## Priests

However large the mosque the mullah only preaches what he knows. *Turkish*

Three things I shall never see: the eye of an ant, the foot of a snake, or the kindness of a mullah. *Persian*

111

A bad doctor destroys your health, a bad mullah destroys your faith. *Turkish*

## Property

Property owned in another town belongs neither to you nor your children. *Arabic*

The man who owns one ear of the camel has a right to make it kneel. *Lebanese*

A house is the first thing bought and the last thing sold. *Arabic*

Land is better than money. *Omani*

## Propriety

Gardeners do not flirt in gardens. *Afghani*

## Protection

The snake-charmer is not immune from snakes. *Medieval Arabic*

## Prostitution

The whore who repents becomes a madame. *Arabic*

Stone never melts, whores never repent. *Tunisian*

It is all right to make an enemy of a woman of good birth, but be very careful when dealing with a whore. *Arabic*

Like a bucket in the public bath, use a whore but pass her on. *Arabic*

## Proverbs

Proverbs are the beacons of conversation. *Arabic*

Proverbs season our speech. *Arabic*

To avoid mistakes, take account of the proverbs. *Turkish*

Better a neat lie than a sloppy truth. *Lebanese*

## Providence

Providence is blind. *Arabic*

Man thinks, God arranges. *Arabic*

The camel has one opinion, the rider another, but God's will prevails over both. *Arabic*

The wind always blows from the wrong direction. *Saudi Arabian*

One sheep, one skin. *Turkish*

Those favoured of fortune can raise fire from snow. *Syrian*

To be singled out for advancement is a misfortune. *Medieval Arabic*

The child who is to die at the age of nine will not die at the age of ten. *Lebanese*

If you don't have a camel, load your bull and trust in
God. *Arabic*

God takes the pulse and prescribes. *Arabic*

God gives of his bounty to the worst of creation. *Lebanese*

At the birth of a kid grass sprouts on the mountain.
*Turkish*

For the birds that cannot soar God has provided low
branches. *Turkish*

For every bean full of weevils God supplies a blind
grocer. *Arabic*

God provides the dervish with a kitchen. *Persian*

(*Note* A dervish is a mendicant monk.)

The blind bird's nest is made by God. *Arabic*

God destroys the tree that does not shade its trunk.
*Arabic*

God gives beans to those with no teeth. *Arabic*

God gives nuts to those with no teeth. *Arabic*

God supplies a blind tailor for every broken needle.
*Lebanese*

God blesses the hairy man and the smooth woman.
*Tunisian*

God looks after children and drunks. *Maltese*

When I sink I am eaten by fish, and when I float I am
eaten by birds. *Omani*

114

If the whole country were made of porridge, the poor would never have more than a spoonful. *Afghani*

There is a road where one rides, there is a place where one lives. *Turkish*

You sow, another reaps. *Moroccan*

Between sunset and the evening prayer God does whatever he pleases. *Tunisian*

When it's noon for me, it's midnight for you. *Arabic*

The last hole of the fox is the furrier's shop. *Arabic*

The cobbler must go barefoot, the weaver must go naked. *Arabic*

*See also*   Destiny, Fate


## Prudence

Do not think too far ahead lest you fall close by. *Arabic*

Never sit where someone can tell you to move. *Arabic*

Never throw stones in the well you take water from. *Saudi Arabian*

If you talk about wolves, have a club handy. *Medieval Arabic*

He who lives in a glass castle should not throw stones. *Moorish*

Never trust a bull, even when his head is in the oven. *Omani*

115

Never ask questions about kings. *Lebanese*

Never adopt a child, never allow a policeman to be a godfather, and never tell your wife what you know. *Maltese*

When I saw the mirage I threw away my water; now I have no water and no mirage. *Arabic*

*See also* Precautions

## Punishment

Punishment rights no wrongs, but it deters a hundred others. *Arabic*

A sword is best used on the man for whom words mean nothing. *Syrian*

He who sows plots reaps poverty. *Yemeni*

The mason was guilty and they hanged the saddler. *Lebanese*

## Purity

The man who is pure of intent can sleep in the road. *Tunisian*

Every scholar makes mistakes, and every thoroughbred stumbles. *Arabic*

If your intentions are pure, how can you be harmed by an ass's fart? *Omani*

## Purpose

He who walks is a bird, he who sits is a stone. *Yemeni*

Conceal all your desires and you will achieve your aims.
*Moroccan*

*See also* Resolution

# R

### Rank

Better an ant's head than a lion's tail. *Maltese*

If I am a prince and you are a prince, who will lead the donkey? *Arabic*

### Rebukes

A friendly warning, delivered in public, is a reprimand. *Arabic*

Two blows on the head hurt. *Arabic*

### Reciprocation

He who spits in your palm, spit in his beard. *Arabic*

I gave him the plague, he gave me pneumonia. *Maltese*

If someone steps on your foot, step on his neck. *Lebanese*

If you throw a bomb to the north, it will land in the south. *Maltese*

If you want peace in your own house don't go banging on your neighbour's door. *Turkish*

We coveted their sheep, they stole our camels. *Saudi Arabian*

Whoever loves you, love him back, even if he is black; whoever pushes you, push him, even at the ravine's edge; whoever insults you, insult him, even if he is descended from the Prophet himself. *Arabic*

### Recognition

An animal is recognised by its dung. *Lebanese*

### Recompense

When the elephant dies there is money in his bones. *Tunisian*

### Recrimination

Do not keep very careful accounts with others or God will keep very careful accounts with you. *Arabic*

Beat the innocent until the guilty confess. *Arabic*

### Reflected glory

The cities are praised, the villages jump for joy. *Medieval Arabic*

### Regrets

I planted an If in the valley of It Was and there grew I Would It Were. *Syrian*

## Relatives

*General*

Relations are scorpions. *Tunisian*

Not all the fingers of a hand are the same length. *Arabic*

My brother and I against my cousin, my cousin and I against the stranger. *Arabic*

Better to choose your wife from the stable than from amongst your relatives. *Lebanese*

A family of seven is never satisfied. *Arabic*

Your family may chew you, but they will not swallow you. *Arabic*

Your relatives may eat your flesh but they will not break your bones. *Lebanese*


*Ancestors*

Always walk proudly in the land of your fathers. *Arabic*


*Brothers*

There is no strength in the legs of a brotherless man. *Persian*

A man's love for a woman waxes and wanes, but his love for a brother is as constant as the stars, as constant as the word of the Prophet. *Arabic*

Another child can be born, another husband can be wed, but a brother lost is lost forever. *Arabic*

120

No one can make you suffer like a brother. *Medieval Arabic*

My brother's wound to me is like a little hole in the wall. *Lebanese*

Your brother is he with whom you get along, not the son of your father and mother. *Tunisian*

Right or wrong, support your brother. *Arabic*

He who digs a pit for his brother will fall into it. *Arabic*

Do not trust a younger brother. *Arabic*

Better an old friend than a new brother. *Arabic*

A single twig cannot make a fire and a single brother cannot take revenge. *Arabic*

A neighbour near is better than a brother far. *Saudi Arabian*


## Cousins

When the angel of death appears, who does not direct him to his cousin? *Iraqi*


## Daughters

Every daughter is handful of trouble. *Arabic*

When the mother and father are weeds how can the daughter be a saffron root? *Arabic*

When a daughter is born the threshold weeps for forty days. *Arabic*

Send a spoilt daughter out to buy coriander and she will come back seven months pregnant. *Moroccan*

Marry off your daughters and remove the shame from your house. *Iraqi*

The unmarried daughter suffers a broken wing. *Arabic*

When a girl begins to bleed, marry her or bury her. *Lebanese*

## Fathers

Better to be a man's wife than a man's daughter. *Maltese*

A father's wrath is the wrath of God. *Arabic*

The father of him who does not take vengeance is an ass. *Lebanese*

The father of daughters does not sleep well. *Arabic*

## Grandsons

The son of your son is your son; the son of your daughter is not. *Iraqi*

## Husbands

One husband is worth seven sons. *Turkish*

## Mothers

He who asks questions about his mother will discover no good. *Maltese*

It is better that a thousand mothers should weep than that mine should shed a single tear. *Lebanese*

Even if the sun shines all day and the lamp burns all night, the house without a mother is dark. *Arabic*

He whose mother is in the house will eat with oil. *Tunisian*

The mother of an impotent male neither rejoices nor grieves. *Arabic*

Whoever marries mother, him will I call Uncle. *Maltese*

Sell your mother and buy a good rifle. *Saudi Arabian*


## Mothers-in-law

A mother-in-law is cold iron fallen to earth. *Arabic*

Inscribed on the gates of Paradise: No daughter-in-law ever loved her mother-in-law. *Lebanese*

A mother-in-law is a fever, a sister-in-law is a poisonous serpent. *Lebanese*

Among a thousand daughters-in-law, one may love her mother-in-law; among two thousand mothers-in-law, one may cherish her daughter-in-law. *Lebanese*

He who bothers to hit his mother-in-law may as well break open her head. *Algerian*


## Nephews

Every nephew is his uncle's enemy. *Lebanese*

123

### Sisters

Two scorpions in a small cave are better than two sisters in the house. *Arabic*

The serpent doesn't bite its sister. *Moroccan*

My sister by my mother is honey in the mouth; my sister by my father is a wind in the reeds. *Tunisian*

### Sons

Your husband is what you make of him; your son is how you raise him. *Arabic*

An ungrateful son is a wart on his father's face. *Afghani*

(*Note*   A longer version of this proverb continues: 'To leave him alone means a blemish, to cut him off means pain.')

It is better to make your son cry than to cry over him. *Arabic*

When your son grows up, make him your brother. *Arabic*

### Step-mothers

Step-mothers are anger sent by God: they neither love nor can be loved. *Arabic*

If my step-mother loves me, she makes me sleep near the oven; if she doesn't, she gives me the leftovers. *Lebanese*

(*Note*   An obscurer version of this proverb goes: 'If my

step-mother loves me she sends me to the oven; if she
doesn't love me – she sends me to the oven.')

*Uncles*

The maternal uncle is like the mule: he doesn't plough,
and he doesn't bequeath. *Tunisian*

The mule says the horse is his uncle. *Lebanese*

## Religion

God gives refuge from the word 'I'. *Tunisian*

The birds praise God, so why shouldn't I? *Persian*

The hunter and the hunted alike call on God. *Turkish*

What belongs to a mosque is unnecessary for a chapel.
*Turkish*

The holiest land, the dirtiest people. *Lebanese*

Balance each hour given to this world with an hour given
to the next. *Arabic*

Fast and pray, and misfortune shall befall you. *Lebanese*

Before it dies every dog shits on the wall of the
mosque. *Turkish*

God helps those who curse religion. *Lebanese*

## Remarriage

Who would tie a donkey in the place of a horse?
*Moroccan*

## Rent

Rent lies with you in bed at night and rises before you in the morning. *Maltese*

*See also* Home

## Repentance

Fast comes the arrow, faster comes revenge, but fastest comes repentance. *Persian*

When a dancer repents her shoulders continue to sway. *Arabic*

## Reproaches

Reproaches are as soap to the heart. *Syrian*

## Republicanism

Among republicans the superior man is chided for being a tyrant. *Persian*

## Reputation

A good name is the fruit of life. *Arabic*

A lost eye is better than a lost reputation. *Turkish*

## Resilience

The man upon whom words have no effect is proof against the stick. *Arabic*

Put a dog's tail in a hollow cane for forty days and it will still come out crooked. *Arabic*

## Resolution

Strike with the sword and rest in its shadow. *Arabic*

Nail drives out nail. *Turkish*

When the hands are strong the eyes are dry. *Arabic*

*See also*   Purpose

## Respect

A man is respected in proportion to how well he dresses. *Arabic*

No one gains respect by playing with slaves or children. *Persian*

To become valuable one must either die or embark on a long journey. *Persian*

He who knew you as a child will have no respect for you as an adult. *Arabic*

## Restraint

He who loves me has not built me a palace; he who hates me has not dug my grave. *Moroccan*

## Reticence

Good men carry their hearts on their tongues; prudent men carry their tongues in their hearts. *Turkish*

Even if words were jewels, silence would be preferable.
*Maltese*

If you tell your troubles to a neighbour you will fall under the axe. *Arabic*

Never say what you think in another man's house, never open a door, and never ask questions. *Maltese*

Do not censure or praise until a year and a half have passed. *Tunisian*

Flies cannot enter the mouth which is closed. *Moroccan*

Beware the silent dog. *Arabic*

*See also* Silence


## Retribution

He who sows evil reaps remorse. *Arabic*

Take the thief before he takes you. *Arabic*


## Revenge

Blood washes away blood. *Arabic*

Vengeance erases shame. *Arabic*

He who takes revenge before a year is out has been quick. *Moroccan*

Mercy is rare, vengeance is common. *Arabic*

The man who does not take revenge is the nephew of an ass. *Sudanese*

128

He who sells you for beans, sell him for their pods. *Tunisian*

If a man has sworn vengeance on you, still you may sleep; but if a woman has sworn vengeance, watch through the night. *Moroccan*

Break one jar of mine and I will break one hundred of yours. *Arabic*

The price of a dog's blood is a dog. *Lebanese*

The grass grows quickly over blood that has been shed honourably. *Kurdish*

If you dig a grave for your neighbour, measure it for yourself. *Turkish*

The tyranny of a Turk is better than the justice of an Arab. *Arabic*

(*Note* The word 'Arab' in this proverb refers to Bedouin.)

## Rewards

The man who plants thistles will reap grapes. *Lebanese*

## Righteousness

The cat which eats her kittens swears they look like mice. *Turkish*

## Risk

He who flees loss flees profit. *Arabic*

129

# S

## Salvation

If all men did not make hasty judgments, all men would go to heaven. *Lebanese*

## Sea, the

Nothing good ever came out of the sea. *Arabic*

The sea takes half the world and seeks the rest. *Tunisian*

The sea is a traitor: he who enters it is lost, he who escapes it is reborn. *Arabic*

Have nothing to do with the sea, even if there is grass growing on its back. *Tunisian*

Until you have seen the sea, commit yourself to nothing. *Turkish*

## Secrets

It is better to part with your head than to part with a secret. *Turkish*

When a secret is shared it is known to all. *Arabic*

The eye that does not see you cannot blame you. *Omani*

A secret is like a dove: when it leaves my hand it takes wing. *Yemeni*

Riding a camel, he thinks no one can see him. *Lebanese*

Your virtues are in your hand, your vices in your armpit. *Persian*

Three things cannot be kept secret: love, pregnancy and riding a camel. *Arabic*

## Self

It is better to escape from oneself than it is to escape from a lion. *Syrian*

## Self-control

If you see two people in harmony, one of them is bearing the burden. *Tunisian*

If you miss a meal, say you are satisfied; if you miss the news, say you have heard it. *Tunisian*

## Self-criticism

What camel ever saw its own hump? *Arabic*

Does the man whose nose stinks cut it off? *Omani*

When a door does not open to your knock, consider your reputation. *Syrian*

## Self-deception

If the camel were to see his own hump, he would fall down and break his neck. *Arabic*

131

## Self-employment

To sell things on one's own doorstep is pure gold.
*Maltese*

Better to tread the pedal of your own loom than the threshold of a master's house. *Arabic*

## Self-importance

Bragging abroad is like singing in the bath. *Turkish*

## Self-improvement

Learn tact from those who lack it. *Lebanese*

## Self-interest

Every prophet prays for his own soul. *Kurdish*

They may be brothers, but their pockets are not sisters. *Turkish*

The blow that falls on someone else falls like a straw. *Syrian*

Everyone pulls the blanket to his side of the bed. *Lebanese*

## Self-reliance

Only the tent pitched by your own hands will stand. *Arabic*

What you cannot arrange for yourself will not be arranged for you. *Arabic*

Use your own brains, for no one else will lend you his. *Arabic*

## Separation

Separation from the living is harder than separation from the dead. *Arabic*

## Servants

The master in his own house is always a guest of his servants. *Turkish*

When the falcon is no longer any use, its feathers stink. *Medieval Arabic*

If a man has a cook, why should he burn his fingers? *Arabic*

Pay your servant before his sweat dries. *Arabic*

There's no need to goad a moving donkey. *Arabic*

Starve your dog and it will follow you. *Arabic*

A servant owes her jewels to God – and her swift tongue. *Arabic*

It is unbearable that one person should rule another. *Lebanese*

One blow from the hand of the master rather than ten blows from his subordinate. *Tunisian*

## Shame

Do not carry your shame to the top of a mountain. *Arabic*

Hide your shame in your house. *Arabic*

Spit in the face of a shameless man and he will tell you it is raining. *Lebanese*

Bribery makes the judge take down his trousers. *Lebanese*

## Sight

The eyes are the spoons of speech. *Arabic*

## Silence

The best medicine for the heart is silence. *Arabic*

The fruit of silence is tranquillity. *Arabic*

To keep silence is response enough. *Syrian*

*See also* Reticence

## Simplicity

The greatest luxury is simplicity. *Kurdish*

## Skills

If skills could be acquired just by watching, every dog would be a butcher. *Turkish*

A craft is a bracelet of gold. *Arabic*

The master of a craft is better than a master of a castle. *Egyptian*

The man who can make you a pin can make you a needle. *Arabic*

Worth as much as a mason among Bedouin. *Arabic*

## Slander

The wounds of the tongue cut deeper than the wounds of the sword. *Arabic*

## Slaves

The slave refuses to sleep for fear that he will dream of domination. *Arabic*

Dominion over slaves is a contemptible thing. *Medieval Arabic*

A slave is a slave, even when he is the master. *Arabic*

## Sleep

Sleep is a Sultan. *Arabic*

Sleep does not come to the cold, the hungry or the fearful. *Syrian*

To sleep is to feast. *Persian*

## Slumming

He who mixes with bran will be eaten by chickens. *Lebanese*

## Smiles

Not every smile is a smile of welcome. *Arabic*

## Snakes

If God had not known what to expect of a snake he would not have put its feet in its belly. *Arabic*

If a snake loves you, wear him as a necklace. *Egyptian*

## Solitude

Solitude is the nest of thoughts. *Kurdish*

Eat alone and cough alone. *Arabic*

## Sorrow

Happiness is a dream, sorrow lasts a year. *Arabic*

## Speech

A man's tongue is his sword. *Arabic*

When the mind is overwhelmed, all words fail. *Arabic*

Say what you like, then hear what you don't like. *Turkish*

There is no tax on talk. *Lebanese*

You spoke, you farted – Wouldn't it have been better not to have spoken? *Lebanese*

Sweet words lure the snake from his hole. *Turkish*

The tongue has no bone, but it crushes bone. *Arabic*

A woman's word is wind in the wind, a man's word is rock in the wall. *Moroccan*

When you speak, do not fear; when you fear, do not speak. *Iraqi*

### Spinsters

Everything that falls is picked up by someone, and even spinsters may sometimes get lucky. *Omani*

### Spoils

You can't divide a piece of shit in two. *Lebanese*

### Strangers

When you shake hands with a stranger count your fingers. *Persian*

Better prison with a friend than the garden with a stranger. *Persian*

### Stupidity

A third of the world is desert locked up in the human brain. *Moroccan*

His upper storey is rented. *Lebanese*

A foolish head makes for weary feet. *Arabic*

To buy a winepress he sold his vineyard. *Arabic*

Looking for his son, his son was sitting on his shoulders.
*Arabic*

He flies from the drain and discovers the gutter. *Syrian*

## Success

Success depends on a man's reputation, not his soul.
*Turkish*

## Sudan

When God made the Sudan he laughed. *Arabic*

## Suggestibility

When one fig tree looks at another both bear fruit.
*Medieval Arabic*

## Suitability

If you love, love a moon; if you steal, steal a camel.
*Egyptian*

## Summer

Wide is the carpet of summer. *Arabic*

The stones of summer may be useful in winter. *Arabic*

Summer is the father of the poor. *Kurdish*

138

## Superstition

Once bitten by a snake, afraid of a trailing rope. *Arabic*

## Survival

People who live on promontories know how to swim. *Arabic*

When the whole pack howls at you, turn and howl with it. *Arabic*

It is the fat mouse that escapes the rat. *Moorish*

Flies know well the sweet-seller's beard. *Lebanese*

All roads lead to the mill. *Syrian*

## Sycophancy

Kiss the hand you cannot bite, and pray for it to be broken. *Arabic*

When the wealthy man eats snake, people say how wise! When the poor man eats snake, people say how foolish! *Arabic*

When you have a favour to ask of a dog, call him 'My Lord'. *Arabic*

Until you are over the river, call your ass 'Sir'. *Moorish*

# T

### Tact

Do not talk of colour to the blind. *Turkish*

### Taste

One man wonders at the work of God, another at the stitching on his coat. *Afghani*

### Taxation

Eat me like a lion, don't worry me like a dog. *Moroccan*

### Tears

If the child does not cry who will give it suck? *Turkish*

The man to make you laugh is the man to make you cry. *Maltese*

### Terror

When the falcon cries no other bird sings. *Arabic*

### Thieves

Whenever the band plays there is always someone stealing the prickly pears. *Maltese*

The thief wins over the miser. *Moorish*

The man who steals a needle will steal a cow. *Arabic*

*See also* Crime

### Thirst

With nothing to drink the world is a field of ruins. *Syrian*

### Thoroughness

When you kill a snake be sure to smash its head. *Iraqi*

### Thought

The man who doesn't know how to think doesn't know how to live. *Arabic*

### Threats

Milking yields milk, pressure yields blood. *Moroccan*

### Thrift

Able to make a wine-cellar out of a raisin. *Lebanese*

### Time

Time is longer than a sausage. *Maltese*

Time rides on the back of a mare. *Arabic*

Time passes by without a word, greeting no one. *Arabic*

When the times you complain of are gone you will weep for them. *Arabic*

A sponge for the past, a rose for the present, a kiss for the future. *Arabic*

Place no faith in time. *Moroccan*

Everything fat will become thin, and everything that flies will come to the earth. *Tunisian*

Wealth softens and misfortune wears out. *Arabic*

When the flood recedes the mud remains. *Turkish*

*See also* Transience


## Tomorrow

Who has seen tomorrow? *Arabic*


## Trades

A fellow craftsman is your brother, even if he is your enemy. *Arabic*

A fellow craftsman is your enemy, even if he is your brother. *Arabic*

The carpenter's door is always broken. *Saudi Arabian*

What time does a tailor have for his own clothes? *Turkish*

She whose father is a goldsmith wears a necklace of gold. *Arabic*

*See also* Skills

## Traditions

O God, do not trim a single custom from us! *Arabic*

Old silk is better than new wool. *Arabic*

## Transience

Lak! lak! cries the stork, and his days are gone. *Turkish*

There is no security in three things: the sea, the Sultan and time. *Arabic*

The moth whirls and whirls, and is then consumed by fire. *Tunisian*

In the end, everything is consumed by moths. *Arabic*

There is no security in either time or money. *Tunisian*

Sleep follows the drawing of the breath just as it follows the rocking of the cradle. *Persian*

Everything in this world is cut short, except the long speech. *Arabic*

## Travel

Travel is a blessing. *Arabic*

Only with travel can a man ripen. *Persian*

Journeys should not begin or end on a Tuesday or a Friday. *Arabic*

No-one goes to the bath or the prison unless he has done what those places imply. *Moroccan*

Choose your companions, then choose your road. *Arabic*

When April comes you can make your bed on the sea. *Moorish*

Every journey is a little piece of Hell. *Tunisian*

When you enter a town swear by its gods. *Arabic*

Every new language mastered is worth a new man. *Lebanese*

To know a people's language is to be safe from their malice. *Lebanese*

Before arriving in a new town, try out its onions. *Lebanese*

Every stranger is a blindman. *Lebanese*

Always travel with someone stronger than you are. *Omani*

Live in any community for forty days and you will become a member. *Arabic*

Have a friend in every town. *Arabic*

To the man who has lost his way a dog's bark is sweeter than a nightingale. *Turkish*

Never ask directions from an inn-keeper. *Turkish*

Praise all other towns, but live in Jaen. *Moorish*

Camels are ships of the land. *Arabic*

Away from home you can tell as many lies as you wish.
*Arabic*

Never travel with a young boy, for if your donkey
stumbles he will ridicule you, and if his donkey
stumbles he will scream. *Lebanese*

When you return from a journey always give a present,
even if it is only a stone. *Iraqi*

### Treachery

Always stroke the head you wish to cut off. *Arabic*

### Trust

Don't trust others, but don't trust yourself either. *Arabic*

### Truth

Truth is the salt of mankind. *Arabic*

The eye of the sun cannot be hidden in a sieve. *Tunisian*

He who speaks the truth must not pitch his tent near
ours. *Tunisian*

Never tell the truth unless you already have one foot in
the stirrup. *Turkish*

A known mistake is better than an unknown truth.
*Arabic*

145

Truth is the daughter of search. *Arabic*

Even from a crooked chimney the smoke rises straight.
*Turkish*

*See also*   Lies, Wisdom


## Turkish

Adam and Eve spoke Persian, but the angel who
expelled them from Paradise spoke Turkish. *Persian*

Questions in Turkish should be answered in Turkish.
*Persian*


## Turks

Where the Turk rides grass will not grow. *Turkish*

# U

### Uncertainty

Towards God's Gate! *Arabic*

(*Note* A very common saying, used in response to the questions, 'Where are you going, what are you doing?')

### Uncountable

There are four things a man cannot count: his sins, his years, his debts, and his enemies. *Persian*

The fish in the sea are not to be counted. *Arabic*

### Unfair!

We taught them to pray, and they got to the mosque ahead of us. *Arabic*

### Unwillingness

When asked to fly the ostrich says he is a camel; when asked to carry a load, the ostrich says he is a bird. *Sudanese*

### Uselessness

A horseman without arms is like a bird without wings. *Arabic*

He who cannot harm cannot help. *Arabic*

No arm for work, no face to beg. *Moroccan*

# V

## Vagabonds

If a dog's prayers were answered the sky would rain bones. *Turkish*

The dog that steals doesn't bite. *Moroccan*

The dog is the jackal's brother. *Arabic*

A dog's life is a long life. *Tunisian*

## Values

What is dust to some is gunpowder to others. *Afghani*

## Vanity

The length of the beard may weaken the brain. *Arabic*

Even when he is dying man wants his coffin to be made of walnut. *Turkish*

## Vice

To contemplate vice is a vice. *Arabic*

## Visiting

Visit your friend when you are hungry, not when you are naked. *Syrian*

The man who does not visit me in time of war will not be welcome in time of peace. *Arabic*

## Volubility

Rich in mouth is poor in hand. *Arabic*

## Vulnerability

A man may worship fire for a hundred years, but still he will burn. *Persian*

# W

### War

The world began with war and will end with war. *Arabic*

Distant drum, sweet music. *Turkish*

Only those afraid of being called cowards make war. *Omani*

War is fun to watch. *Omani*

War is easy to watch through field glasses. *Lebanese*

Every non-fighter recommends war. *Omani*

Numbers overcome the brave. *Arabic*

### Watchmen

A watchman is the guarantee of peace. *Tunisian*

### Wealth

Wealth is an unguent. *Arabic*

Wealth is a veil that covers man's shame. *Arabic*

Too much wealth makes a man blind. *Arabic*

He who seeks wealth without capital is like the man who carries water in a sieve. *Arabic*

He who has gold can do what he likes. *Arabic*

The heart of the rich man is always weary. *Arabic*

Never pray for your friend to become wealthy, for you will lose him. *Arabic*

Wealth sends people to Hell. *Arabic*

He who beats on the door of Hell beats with a golden hammer. *Arabic*

A man with money can eat sherbet in Hell. *Arabic*

Any door opens to keys of gold. *Arabic*

Everyone sides with the rich. *Lebanese*

The wealthy are addressed with songs, the poor are addressed with stones. *Arabic*

A single source of income is bad. *Arabic*

When the poor man says a mouse has eaten the leather fittings on his ploughshare he will be called a liar, but when the rich man says the mouse has eaten his ploughshare he tells the truth. *Lebanese*

Better an abundance of children than an abundance of chattels. *Arabic*

Every treasure has its demon. *Moroccan*

I am sick of the oil of anchovies! *Omani*

*See also* Money, Poverty

152

## Weapons

There is no faith in women, horses or swords. *Persian*

## Weather

A day of cloud is for hunting, a day of wind is for sleeping, a day of rain is for entertaining, and day of sun is for trade. *Arabic*

## Wedding expenses

He who incurs a debt to get married will have to sell his children to pay the interest. *Lebanese*

## West, the

Nothing coming from the West rejoices the heart. *Egyptian*

## Winter

On a winter's day the fireside is a bed of tulips. *Turkish*

## Wisdom

The words of the ancients are wisdom. *Arabic*

Ask a man of experience, not a physician. *Tunisian*

The wise are always at peace. *Arabic*

The wise man speaks of what he sees, the idiot of what he hears. *Arabic*

Forty wise men cannot recover a stone thrown into the sea by a fool. *Turkish*

A wise man's guess is truer than a fool's certainty. *Arabic*

*See also* Learning, Truth

## Wolves

The wolf-cub is always ill-licked. *Egyptian*

## Women

God has omitted women from his mercy. *Arabic*

Women are hell, but still no house should be without them. *Persian*

Women always leave their intelligence at home. *Kurdish*

A woman is only ever well inside her house and inside her grave. *Afghani*

Women and motorcycles, joy and grief. *Maltese*

Even if a woman's candlestick is cast in gold, still it is the man who must supply the candle. *Turkish*

A slave thinks of nothing but escape until he dies, a woman of nothing but divorce. *Sudanese*

If it were not for shame, there would be no honest women. *Arabic*

As soon as your daughter can lift a cup to her mouth she wants what her mother wants. *Moorish*

Don't call a woman a whore while her mother is still in the house. *Omani*

You can't fill your belly with beauty. *Arabic*

Obedience to women leads to Hell. *Tunisian*

Life is full of unhappiness and most of it caused by women. *Lebanese*

A single woman destroyed Paradise. *Arabic*

A single piece of wood cannot make a fire and a single woman cannot run a house. *Arabic*

I sprinkled her with rose water, she sprinkled me with shit. *Moorish*

Intelligence is the ornament of every serious woman. *Lebanese*

Trust not in kings, horses, or women. *Persian*

The tall woman gets what she wants, the short woman yells at her neighbour. *Arabic*

The woman with no purse is a shameful thing. *Arabic*

There is someone to pick up every fallen woman. *Lebanese*

If I had relied on you, O husband, we would never have had children. *Moroccan*

When white women quarrel, they pull each other's hair out: when black women quarrel, blood flows. *Moroccan*

No man is less than any woman. *Arabic*

155

The thicker the veil, the less worth lifting. *Turkish*

Behind veils is poison. *Arabic*

A woman without a veil is like food without salt. *Afghani*

After thirty years the woman says, What's the matter, husband, you only have one eye. *Tunisian*

The woman who smiles at you seeks to deceive you; the woman who weeps has already done so. *Arabic*

For beauty, a Georgian; for wiles, a Jewess; for peace, a Christian; for pride and fantasy, a Turk; for nobleness and generosity, an Arab woman. *Algerian*

When the hen crows like a cock, kill it. *Arabic*

What the devil may accomplish in a year, an old woman may accomplish in an hour. *Moroccan*

*See also*   Girls, Male and female, Men

## Work

Hard work means a long life but short days. *Turkish*

Work is prayer. *Arabic*

He who works hard is the equal of he who fights in the Holy War. *Arabic*

Hands perish, but not their work. *Arabic*

Too much work only earns a bad hernia. *Lebanese*

He who works eats. *Arabic*

He who works hardest eats least. *Maltese*

The needle conquers the weaver. *Lebanese*

## World, the

The world is a mother. *Lebanese*

## Worries

The only worry-free head is a scarecrow's. *Turkish*

I went to Damascus to get rid of my worries. Damascus was full of worries. *Lebanese*

*See also* Anxiety

# Y

### Year, the

A bad year has twenty-four months. *Lebanese*

### Youth

The old treat you with courtesy, but the young drive you insane. *Maltese*

Neither Sultan nor Beg can stand in youth's way. *Arabic*

(*Note* A beg, or bey, was a provincial governor in the Ottoman Empire.)